Walks on the
Isle of Skye

Publisher's Note

This completely new edition of this popular book contains a
number of walks from the first edition, which have been
thoroughly updated and some routes extended. It contains a
considerable number of enjoyable new walks, some more
challenging, all delightful. A few have been omitted.

If, in spite of the authors' efforts, readers find anything
incorrect or misleading in the text we shall be glad to be
informed for future reference. However, it must be stated that
the book sets out to be an entertaining and helpful guide, and
neither the authors nor the publishers can be held responsible
for any loss or injury that might be considered to result from
its use.

Finally we would set down our delight to have Mary Welsh's
eleven Scottish Walks titles under our own imprint and
published in Scotland. We are also pleased to have, in this
edition, Christine Isherwood's collaboration in the research plus
the indispensable enhancement of her maps and illustrations.

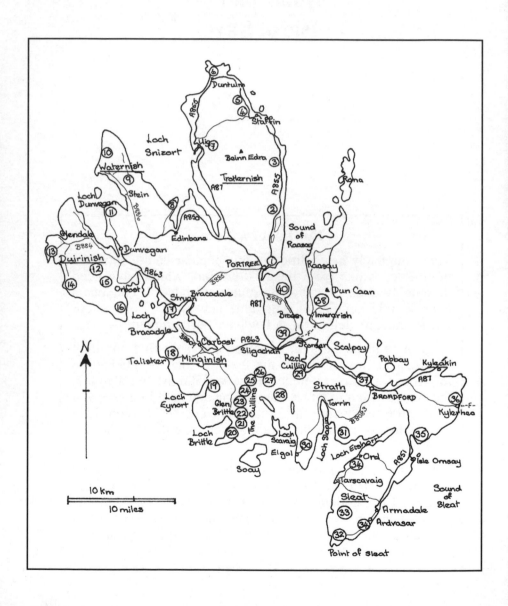

Clan Walk Guides

Walks on the Isle of Skye

Mary Welsh
and
Christine Isherwood

First Published by Westmorland Gazette 1990

Revised Edition Published by Clan Books 2000

New Edition Published by Clan Books 2002

ISBN 1 873597 17 7

Text and Illustrations
© Mary Welsh
and
Christine Isherwood
2001

Clan Books
Clandon House
The Cross, Doune
Perthshire
FK16 6BE

Printed by
Cordfall Ltd, Glasgow

Contents

contents continued page 4

The Lump and Ben Chracaig from Portree

From the Skye bridge take the A87 to Portree. On the edge of the town, pass the Aros Experience and then the High School, on the left. Here follow the A855, curving right. Almost immediately take, on the right, the signed long stay car park, grid ref. 482436.

On nearing **Portree**, look on its signboard for its name in Gaelic, 'Port-an-Righ'—the Port of the King. Once the settlement was called Kiltaraglen, which means the Chapel at the foot of the Glen. But in 1540 King James V, at the head of his fleet, sailed round the island and then dropped anchor in the harbour. In what is now Portree's Somerled Square the Clan Chiefs made their submission to the King, justice was dispensed, outstanding disputes settled and the village was called, thereafter, Port-an-Righ. Overlooking the harbour is the dramatic 'Lump', where, at the end of August, the Skye Games are held.

The gently sloping sward, rising shelf-like up to the magnificent cliffs of Creag Mhor, is called **The Bile**. It is a raised beach cut by the sea. When the glaciers retreated at the end of the last glacial period the land rose as the weight reduced, and beaches were left 'high and dry'.

Portree Harbour

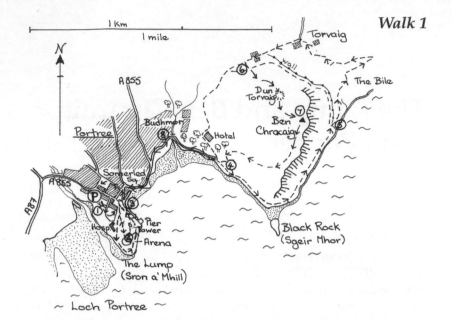

1 Leave the far end of the car park and go left up Bayfield Road. Turn right and then left to pass through an iron gate into the cemetery. Leave it by steps and a gate in the far left corner. Walk right and opposite the Portree Medical Centre take a broad track, on the left, climbing below the fine scots pines of The Lump. The track leads to a natural grassy arena, with rocky outcrops, the site of the Games—a beautiful hollow, with the sparkling waters of Loch Portree glimpsed through the trees.

2 Walk back along the wide way for a few metres and stroll right towards the crenellated Tower. Climb the metal spiral steps for a grand view of the harbour, Ben Tianavaig and of The Storr. Descend and return to the wide track. Turn right and, just before the entrance gate, walk left to stroll a delightful path. Climb the steps and continue along the way that almost encircles the Lump. The path, high above the town, comes close to the edge of some steep slopes—so walk with care and stop to enjoy the glorious views. Continue to the road. Turn right along Bank Street and then descend stone steps, on the right, to continue right along Quay Street to the pier— the latter built by Thomas Telford. Pause here to look for mergansers diving for sand eels, their favourite food.

3 Walk back along the harbourside and climb Quay Brae. Bear right past Safeway's supermarket and then right again along Bosville Terrace and Mill Road. Look away over the loch and ahead to the sculptured side of Ben Tianavaig. Turn right again off the main road and descend Scorrybreac to take a right fork to pass the entrance lane to the Cuillin Hills Hotel. Just beyond, strike right along the signed footpath which continues high above the shoreline. The reinforced path is easy to walk and from it the views of Portree Harbour and The Lump are stunning.

4 Go through a gate and on past a raised area, with a picnic table and a Clan Nicholson Memorial (this is your return route and should be ignored). Go on ahead to wind, north-east, round the headland. Down below is the tidal island of Black Rock. Now Dun Caan on Raasay comes into view. Look ahead to see The Bile and the dramatic cliffs beyond. Follow the good path as it climbs, descends and then levels out to come to a gate in the wall.

5 Pass through and follow the grassy path that bears steadily left to a gate in a fence. Beyond, turn left and climb the pasture to reach a wide grassy track. Walk right along this, with the fence to your left, to go over a stile. Here walk left, away from The Bile, to begin your steady ascent of a wide terraced track. This is excellently graded and a delight to walk, with magnificent views. Pass through a gate to the dwellings at Torvaig. Go across the turning area, bear right and then immediately left down the lane to pass through sheep pens and cattle sheds to a gate and a stile.

6 Turn left just beyond the stile to ascend steadily beside the fence. Climb the next stile and, using sheep trods and animal tracks, climb steadily upward over heather to come to Dun Torvaig, now just a

Mergansers

Black Guillemot

huge cluster of stones on a rocky mound—what a good defensive site was chosen. Descend from the dun in the direction of the sea or wind round its base to follow an indistinct path that leads up onto Ben Chracaig, with its superb view over Loch Portree.

7 After a long pause here, turn right, south-west, to stroll a good path in the direction of Portree. It descends along the cliff edge and eventually curves round the headland high above Black Rock. It goes on downwards, generally easily, with a couple of little scrambles, to wind down and down to the Nicholson memorial, noted earlier. Walk on a few yards to join the outward route. Turn right to walk along Scorrybreac.

8 Go on along Mill Road and Bosville Terrace to turn right along Wentworth Street to reach Somerled Square, which you cross, left. Go over Bridge Road to drop down steps into the car park.

Heath Bedstraw

Practicals

Type of walk: A lovely route, with magnificent views. Very pleasing path all the way to Torvaig. If you do not wish to climb the dun and the cliff top go on along the continuing track, beyond the cattle sheds, to arrive at the outward track beside the entrance lane to the Cuillin Hills Hotel.

Distance: 5 miles / 8 km
Time: 2–3 hours
Map: OS Landranger 23

The Old Man of Storr

Leave Portree by the A855. After six miles watch for the magic moment when first Loch Fada and then Loch Leathan come into view, with the Old Man of Storr and one of its satellites high up on the skyline above. Park in the Forestry car park on the left side of the road, grid ref. 508528.

All paths seem to lead to the bottom of the **Old Man**, a huge pear-shaped leaning pillar of rock, 165ft/50m in height, which is undercut at its base. The landslips were formed when sedimentary rock gradually collapsed under the weight of the basalt lava which had overtopped it. The stacks were probably formed by later erosion. The Old Man was first climbed in 1955 by the late Donald Whillans and is still graded 'Very severe'.

Running along behind the Old Man and other accompanying weird and fantastic pinnacles is the **Storr**

The Old Man of Storr

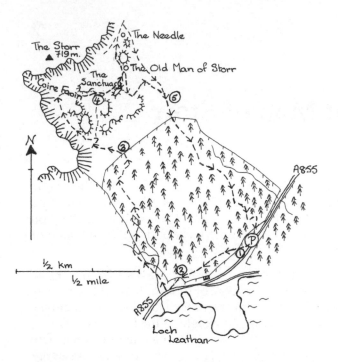

Ridge, the Storr itself reaching 2,360ft/719m above sea-level. This formidable wall of rock, with its stone-floored gullies and its blasted and riven surfaces, shelters the Sanctuary, the basin which in turn shelters the Old Man and other pillars and pinnacles. Wander at will through the Sanctuary, where no rock has been softened by nature or by man.

1 Take the path leading south-west out of the car park. It climbs gradually above the road until it reaches a fence at an old broken stile. Step over the fence and continue on a clear path along a very wide firebreak through trees, crossing two little burns on the way. Go on towards the forest edge, with a wonderful view over Loch Leathan and, in the distance, the Cuillin. Up to the right, between the trees, are glimpses of the Storr.

2 Cross a burn and, just afterwards, bear left to take a kissing gate through the boundary fence thereby avoiding a very boggy area. Follow the fence, right, and then go downhill towards the road. Round a fence corner just above the road and climb a stile back over the fence. Follow a wide grassy swathe uphill. Cross a burn

10

and continue uphill, still outside the fence, with a broken wall beyond it, until a clear firebreak in the trees appears. Here, especially if it is windy, it is worth re-entering the forest and following a path that goes on up. Pass a small fenced enclosure on the drier right side, and then climb on up through larch to a high open valley. Where the path meets spruce trees, turn sharply right, and continue to climb steeply through another open area. The way then passes through more spruce to the fence at the top of the forest, where various paths join.

3 Step over the fence and take the steepish path uphill towards the cliffs. Follow it where it zig-zags upwards towards two great rocky pinnacles. The main path passes steeply between them but this walk takes a less steep path, to the left, that leads up into Coire Faoin. As you get higher into the corrie, wind round right, following one of the many paths which skirts a small hollow and brings you with stunning suddenness above the Sanctuary, with the Old Man of Storr and the other pinnacles arrayed

C.M.Isherwood

Ravens

before you. The huge unstable cliffs of the Storr tower over you on the left.

4 Descend to the path which skirts the Sanctuary. Climb up the base of the Old Man if you wish. Enjoy the peace of this tranquil hollow which is occasionally broken by the croak of a raven. Then choose your way of descent. If you take the good path left (north) you join a large obvious path which turns east and heads off down to the forest. Or you may prefer to go over the col to the right (south) of the Old Man. You then contour round on a less well used path, the haunt of many rabbits, which also descends and zig-zags down the hillside, at an easy angle, to join the 'tourist trail' lower down.

5 Then follow the main path which has been pitched using local stone in an attempt to stop the erosion. Continue on to pass through a kissing gate into the forest. The well drained and well graded path continues through the trees. It has been reconstructed by the Skye and Lochalsh Footpath Trust and is now a delight to walk. It leaves the forest by a stile at an information board at the north end of the car park.

Rabbits

Practicals

Type of walk: This is a steep but straightforward walk, with some fairly wet areas in the forest. The rock scenery is magnificent and the path down is excellent. The landslipped area behind the pinnacles is a maze of hummocks and hollows, with paths running in all directions and could be extremely confusing in the mist.

Distance: 3 miles / 5 km
Time: 3–4 hours
Map: OS Landranger 23

Loch Cuithir and the Lealt Waterfall

Park in the large lay-by parking area, grid ref. 516606, on the east side of the A855, south of the turning to Lealt.

Diatomite is a lake sediment formed from the remains of microscopic alga, rich in silica. It is used in filters, face powder and fire proofing, etc. Loch Cuithir was found to be floored with

Loch Cuithir and Sgurr a' Mhadaidh Ruaidh

diatomite and, in 1886, the water was drained to help with the extraction of this chalk-like substance. It was then carried in wagons along an iron tramway to Inver Tote to be dried before being sent on to Glasgow. Later a road, reputedly the most expensive stretch built in the Highlands, was constructed to replace the railway to help with the extraction and transport of the diatomite. The industry eventually failed to compete with foreign imports though it revived between 1950 and 1961 (see leaflet "In the footsteps of Trades and Industries" obtained from Skye's TICs). Today nature has reclaimed much of the floor of the loch with just three small picturesque lochans remaining.

Sgurr a' Mhadaidh Ruaidh (Red Fox's Peak) towers, pyramid-shaped, above Loch Cuithir, encouraging you on as you approach the lonely pools in the hollow of the hills. It is part of the Trotternish Ridge and from the approach route you can spot The Storr to your left and Ben Edra to the right.

The spectacular **Lealt waterfall** descends into its impressive gorge after dropping over a rocky lip below the level of the A-road. The Lealt then hurries a short distance to the sea at Inver Tote where the diatomite was dried before shipment. The ruins of the old buildings can still be seen.

Sea Eagle

14

1 From the roadside parking, cross the A855, with care. Take narrow road, opposite, signed Lealt, and as you go notice the tra of lazy-beds on either side. From here you can just glimpse 7 Storr and Ben Edra. Ahead, dominating the walk, is the shapely Red Fox's Peak.

2 Beyond the dwellings go on along the road that continues over extensive moorland, with the Lealt River to your left. Keep a wary eye here for a sea eagle, recognised by it huge size and its white tail feathers. After 2 miles/3.2km you reach a point where, on the map, the grassy bed of the dismantled tramway and the road converge. Look right to see Meall na Suiramach and the Quiraing.

3 Continue on the road until you reach the first of the three small lochans and the remnants of buildings. Cross the sturdy footbridge to pass the second and third lochans and on to where the track ends in bog. Stand and enjoy this awesome hollow, almost surrounded by dramatic skirts of basalt and green slopes. Find a sunny bank for your picnic.

4 Return to the footbridge, but do not cross. Walk right along a narrow animal trod, just above a burn. Continue on to the abutments of a tiny bridge that once carried the tramway over a burn. Move left or right to find an easy way over the water and go on. (This is the first of several burns that have lost their bridges and each must be negotiated—but all are crossed easily.) Look ahead from here to

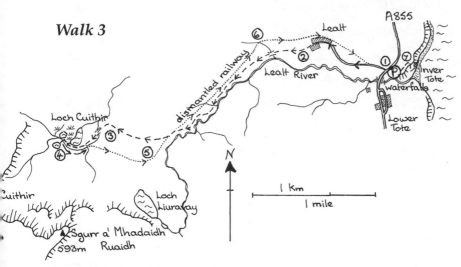

Walk 3

15

see the tramway crossing the moor—a grassy way on a raised causeway, with heather and peat hags stretching away on either side.

5 As you walk enjoy the stunning view, across the Sound of Raasay to Ben Alligin and Liathach in Wester Ross. Go on to join the road taken to reach the loch. Turn right for a 100m and then climb, left, up the banking to see the track—still an embanked causeway, stretching away for as far as the eye can see. On reaching a gate and a fence go on along the right of the latter to keep generally dryshod. As you come upon each boggy area make a short diversion to find a drier way, and then return to the continuing trackbed.

6 At the start of an incline the railway has been colonised by rushes but these are not too dense to prevent you remaining on the tramway. At the top of the incline follow the rushes over flatter featureless moorland, with the houses of Lealt to the right. The track runs parallel with a fence and for a short distance is indistinct. Go on and shortly you can see the way running ahead, with fewer rushes and more grass. Continue until you reach the narrow road walked at the outset. A few yards on cross the A855.

7 From the parking area take the kissing gate, signed "Danger. Keep to footpath". Walk the reinforced way along the edge of the Lealt's great gorge. Pause, just before the path descends a little, to look back at the superb waterfall. At the cliff edge turn right as directed by an arrow. A zig-zagging path leads down to the black beach of Inver Tote Bay and the site of a kiln used by the diatomite works.

8 Return by the same route.

Practicals

Type of walk: A good moorland walk on a sturdy road and a pleasing grassy trackbed, with several little challenges where bridges have 'gone' over small streams. There are dramatic views on the outward journey and magnificent ones on the return. Walk only as far as you are happy to do so on the way to Inver Tote Bay.

Distance: 6½ miles / 12 km
Time: 3–4 hours
Map: OS Landranger 23

The Quiraing
(stronghold or ringed fence)

Park in a lay-by on the highest point of the minor road through the pass between Uig and Staffin, grid ref. 444683.

The Quiraing, the most dramatic part of the Trotternish ridge, lies to the north of the road through the pass. The ridge, huge inland cliffs of volcanic lava, was laid down 60 million years ago. Its eastern slopes are sheer, with landslips and tortured weathered pinnacles of basalt.

*The Quiraing
(the Needle)*

Heather and grass cover the less steep slopes of the Quiraing and among these plants grow wild strawberry and alpine lady's mantle. Close to the path the pretty rose-coloured moss campion thrives. Rose-root flourishes in the many crevices of wide ravines that run down to The Table and in spring purple saxifrage flowers.

Golden Eagles. Many pairs breed successfully on the island and you would be unlucky not to spot one. Do not mistake the smaller buzzard for a golden eagle. When the sun catches the latter's feathers and its size is revealed it is beyond doubt. If your eagle is enormous and has a shortish white tail and a huge head it is likely to be a sea eagle. These birds died out in the nineteenth and early twentieth century but after a successful breeding regime on the island of Rum numbers are increasing. They are regularly seen over Skye.

Walk 4

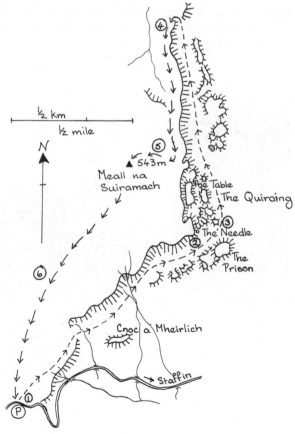

1 Cross the road and follow the wide well used track that skirts a rocky outcrop. From this knoll enjoy the view of Staffin Bay, the Island of Rona and the mountains of Wester Ross. Look down on the hairpin bends of the road through the pass and, beyond, to Loch Cleat and Loch Leum na Luirginn. You can also see the dramatic continuation of the

Moss Campion

Trotternish ridge to Beinn Edra. Follow the path, with the bare hill of Maoladh Mor to your left. The way continues north-east and brings you to a gully. Keep to the inner edge of the path to negotiate this cleft safely and then continue on the path as it hugs the side of the cliff.

2 The way leads you to the bottom of the sheer face of The Prison, a huge mass of rock that looks like a fortress. An eroded path leads up it and edges a sheer drop but it is not a route for the fainthearted or for those with vertigo. On the opposite side of the path stands The Needle, a huge pillar of basalt, the sides of which seem inaccessible to all but the ravens. Below the pinnacle lies a steep slope of scree and grass; by ascending this and then passing left around The Needle, and on up through the cliffs beyond, you can reach The Table. This is a large, oval-shaped bright green table of grass surrounded by towers and pinnacles of rock and castellated crags. It was used in times past for hiding hundreds of cattle (some say as many as 3,000) from raiders—and in modern times for a game of shinty and for car advertisements! Do not despair if you find the badly eroded scree slope too daunting as it can be seen again later on the walk—but it cannot be approached from above.

3 Continue along the path. Climb a short scree slope, then walk on along another narrow path with steepish slopes dropping away to the right. Cross an old fence and walk on, north, along a sometimes muddy path. Ahead lies a quiet, high-level grassy valley, with a pretty lochan. Vertical rock faces lie to the left and huge heather-clad rocky outcrops to the right. Follow the path as it climbs out of the tiny glen, walking towards a col. After crossing the wall at the top of the col, bear left to a cairn.

4 Continue bearing left, climbing steeply through a gully. You are now heading southwards in the direction of Meall na Suiramach. As you climb, the path comes close to the cliff edge and from here you can see several lovely dark blue lochans that were hidden from sight as you walked through the valley, now far below. Also from the edge of the cliff you have an excellent and exciting view down to The Table—but do not attempt a descent.

5 Continue right, uphill, to attain the summit, 1,663ft/543m, which is crowned by a cairn. After enjoying the view strike down and inland over the moorland, well away from the continuing cliff edge. There is no obvious path but aim for a sheep-track on the rocks ahead, remaining on the same contour. Walk on until you are clear of the cliffs and you can see the parking area far below.

6 When in line with it begin to descend the heathery slopes.

Golden Eagle

Practicals

Type of walk: A challenging but breath-taking mountain walk. The Gaelic name for the Isle of Skye translates as the Isle of Mist, and clouds often envelop the high peaks of the island. This is certainly true of Quiraing where the mists can drift down suddenly. Be prepared to turn back.

Distance: 4½ miles / 7.25 km
Time: 3 hours
Map: OS Landranger 23
Terrain: Strenuous walking over rocky and sometimes steep terrain. Good walking boots and waterproof clothing are essential.

The Quiraing, from the north, and Fingal's Pinnacles

Park in the large lay-by, grid ref. 464707, on the A855. It lies north of a small loch with a picnic area, and south of the start of the walk.

The raven, the largest and most intelligent of the crow family, is a great black bird with a large beak and head, and a diamond-shaped tail. It frequently soars and wheels at a considerable height, its wings motionless and its wing feathers extended like fingers. It does superb aerobatics, closing its wings and turning over in the air.

Mossy saxifrage, seen in the more remote parts of this walk, is a pretty tufted plant with white flowers, half an inch across but often much smaller. The plant forms moss-like cushions and the flowering shoots are five or six inches long.

Loch Langaig, Quiraing and Leac nan Fionn

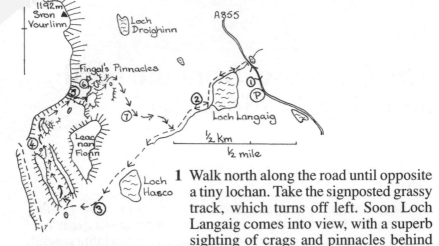

1 Walk north along the road until opposite a tiny lochan. Take the signposted grassy track, which turns off left. Soon Loch Langaig comes into view, with a superb sighting of crags and pinnacles behind it—Quiraing to the left and Sron Vourlinn to the right. Between, and nearer, lies Leac nan Fionn (Fingal's Tombstone). The track follows round the shore of the loch and then goes up by the inflowing burn.

2 Go on where the track diminishes to a good path. Climb steadily through a long valley and then, over a lip, Loch Hasco appears below, secret in its hollow, with no apparent outflow. Continue on the path which stays well above the loch and climbs on a rising traverse across the hillside. Cross the fence by a stile and continue into and across a grassy hollow.

3 Contour round the next hollow, a bouldery one, then climb to a small col, from where you can spot the path running along below the ridge from Quiraing to Meall na Suiramach clearly ahead. At this point, turn right (north) from the col. Follow sheep tracks along the top of the ridge for a very short distance and then zig-zag up the steep slope ahead to a wall. Go round the left end of the wall and walk north into a shallow valley behind Leac nan Fionn. Here look for ravens 'playing' in the updraughts from the cliffs.

4 Descend the bouldery valley to a small pool. Turn left across the marshy area below the pool and follow a path which winds round and down below the first cliffs of Sron Vourlinn. Continue on the path and on along a ridge, with a shallow trough to the left and a tiny lochan to the right. Ahead is a fence and a wall across a col

22

Mossy Saxifrage

between the cliffs of Sron Vourlinn and Leac nan Fionn.

5 Step over the fence and climb through a gap in the wall, keeping towards the lowest part of the col. At this point it appears as if you are about to go over a cliff, but the way down is much easier than it looks. Go down into a tiny hollow and take a path which goes away to the right, descending easily below cliffs into the amazing hollow of the Pinnacle Basin.

6 Explore the superb pinnacles, which are on a slightly smaller scale than those of the Storr Sanctuary. The basin has many little hollows and hummocks and it would be easy to get lost in the mist—be warned. Mossy saxifrage, alpine lady's mantle, roseroot, thyme and stonecrop thrive here in the fertile basalt soil. Then leave this hollow by choosing tracks which lead east to the lip of the basin. Head downwards to the right, making use of sheep tracks and landslip terraces to descend the steep hillside easily on a long slant.

7 Below the final cliff of Leac nan Fionn a more defined path emerges, leading down gentler slopes east to a hollow with a burn. From here you can see the outward path, below and to the right. Go down the heathery slopes to join it and retrace your steps to Loch Langaig and the road.

Practicals

Type of walk: This delightful walk uses an excellent path upwards. Some walkers will want to return by the same route and will definitely do so if mist descends. This walk returns by an interesting way down, visiting a little known and unspoiled area. There are some steep slopes, but nothing too long or too difficult, and no great exposure.

Distance: 5 miles / 8 km
Time: 3–4 hours
Map: OS Landranger 23

6

Duntulm Castle and Rubha Hunish

Park in the large lay-by the entrance path to Duntulm Castle, grid ref. 412742.

The cairn you pass on the way to the ruins of Duntulm Castle is a memorial to **the MacArthurs**, who were hereditary pipers to the castle. The ruins are being restored by a local group and contributions to this work are welcomed. The castle was once the proud stronghold of the MacDonalds, Lords of the Isles. Beyond the ruin the cliffs drop sheer to the sea.

Rubha Hunish (Bear's or Hunn's Point), a peninsula, is the most northerly point on Skye. The best view of it is from the old coastguard lookout hut on the 300ft/100m cliffs. Just east of here

Duntulm Castle

you can look down on the layering of the strata of the cliffs—
below the headland turf it lies aslant and half-way down the cliff
the gigantic columns of basalt drop vertically into the sea. Enjoy
the fine view of the Shiants and the Western Isles.

1 From the parking place by the castle take the path downhill and
through the kissing gate, which is the entrance to the ruin. Follow
the path uphill again and where it turns left along the top of a short
promontory. At the end lies the castle.

Walk 6

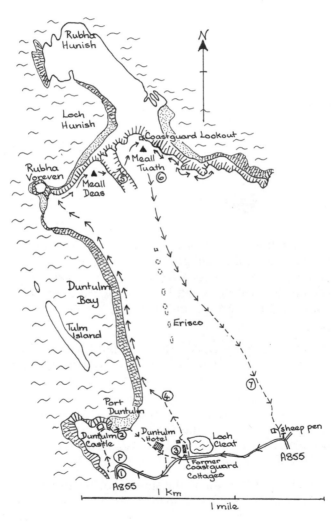

2 From here, take a fenced path on the east side of the headland. This slopes steeply downwards to Port Duntulm, ending in steps to the beach. Cross the black sand and boulder beach. Look across to Tulm Island, where in summer, you might spot a basking shark in the bay. A short distance across the beach, watch out for a track which leads up past the side of Duntulm Castle Hotel. Pass the entrance and take the left turn up to the main road, where you walk left for a short distance.

Basking Shark

3 Take the track which passes in front of a row of holiday cottages (once coastguard cottages) and go through a gate at the end by another cottage. Cross a field corner to a gate, which brings you out just beyond the small Loch Cleat. Turn left, following a good path along by a wall, to climb a rickety stile, a few yards along the fence.

4 Beyond, carry on beside the wall until it turns sharply downhill towards the sea. Then head down more gradually to take a path which picks its way above Tulm Bay. At the far end cross a fence and climb up through heather onto Meall Deas (the South Hill). Follow the path round the western edge of the hill to look down on Rubha Voreven. A little further on you come to a rocky defile between Meall Deas and Meall Tuath (the North Hill, which is the higher of the two).

5 From the defile climb to the summit of Meall Tuath, where you are directly above Rubha Hunish. There is an old coastguard lookout station here from where the views are superb. (At this point you might wish to continue along the cliffs to enjoy more of this very wild coastline).

6 To return, go back towards the coastguard lookout and then, heading away from the cliffs, descend the hill, keeping to the edge of a small escarpment which runs inland across the moor. Partway across and below you on the right, there is a line of old ruined crofts, remains of the settlement of Erisco. The path now becomes more distinct, following the edge with boggier moor below and Tulm Bay, with its island, out to the right. There are good views of the end of the Trottenish ridge with Sgurr Mor and the dramatic cliffs of Sron Vourlinn ahead.

7 The path eventually crosses an old dyke (low turf and stone) and runs along above another. Then it descends from the escarpment to pass to the left of some sheep pens and comes to a stile on to the road by a phone box. Turn right to return to your car.

Cormorant eating fish

Practicals

Type of walk: A visit to an emotive ruin, followed by a wild high level coastal walk with few paths but wide dramatic seascapes.

Distance:	5 miles / 8 km
Time:	2–3 hours
Map:	OS Landranger 23

7

Beinn Edra

Drive northwards along the A87 towards Uig. Cross the bridge over the River Conon and turn right, ascending the single track road that hairpins for much of its first half mile. Continue through Glen Conon to the gate at the end of the road and, beyond, park in a large reinforced lay-by, grid ref. 418637.

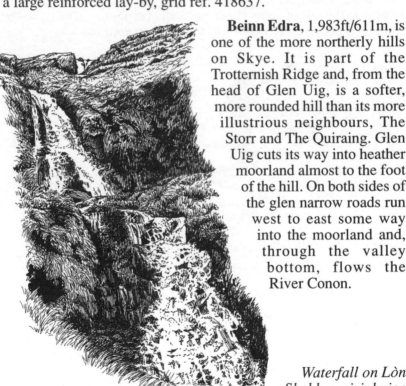

Beinn Edra, 1,983ft/611m, is one of the more northerly hills on Skye. It is part of the Trotternish Ridge and, from the head of Glen Uig, is a softer, more rounded hill than its more illustrious neighbours, The Storr and The Quiraing. Glen Uig cuts its way into heather moorland almost to the foot of the hill. On both sides of the glen narrow roads run west to east some way into the moorland and, through the valley bottom, flows the River Conon.

Waterfall on Lòn Shobhar-airighuige – tributary of River Connon

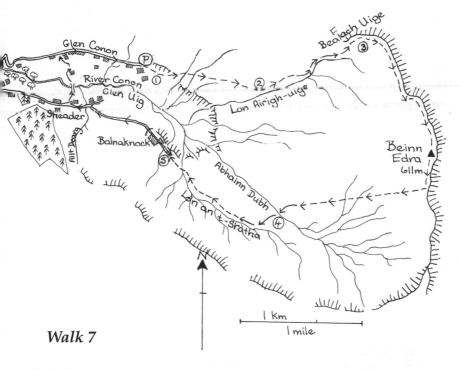

Walk 7

1 Walk on along the gated track to cross several tributaries of the River Conon. The track now swings out onto open moorland where heather, tormentil and eyebright flower in the summer. After a mile the track fades as it comes to the edge of some extensive peat cuttings. Keep well above the latter as you walk to the fence ahead. Cross the fence and walk beside it down to the edge of Lon Airigh-uige, another tributary of the Conon.

2 Do not cross but follow the narrow, faint and sometimes wet path that keeps close to the gurgling stream for most of its length. It is easy to walk and passes through banks of heather. It comes close to the ruins of some old crofts. Climb up past several pretty cascades tumbling though summer gardens of ferns, heather, golden saxifrage, alpine lady's mantle and primroses. Above the falls you have a first dramatic sighting of the Quiraing and of the northerly MacLeod's Table. Go on along a tiny path keeping the stream to your right. It becomes narrower and in places gets lost underground, out of sight but not of sound. Continue climbing the grassy slopes to the ridge, just south of Bealach Uige. Suddenly the views are

stunning of both shores of the peninsula—Uig Bay, the Ascrib Islands, Waternish headland, Staffin Bay and the mainland mountains.

3 Walk south (right) along the ridge for four-fifths of a mile to the trig. point on the domed summit, with more wonderful views in all directions. Continue on from the summit down the ridge for a quarter of a mile to the Bealach a Mhoramhain. Here look down to see a turf dyke stretching straight down the moorland. Follow this to pass through a low band of rocks and then on to cross the Abhainn Dhubh, below the lowest waterfall. If this is not possible, veer left across the boggy tiresome moorland to cross a quarter of a mile above the waterfall.

Primroses

4 From the far side of the river continue ahead using heathery hummocks that project above the bog to reach a track that takes you on towards Balnaknock. The Lon an t-Stratha carries on beside you, on the left, and eventually you have to cross it on well placed large stepping stones. (These might be underwater after heavy rain—so choose a good day.) Continue on the gated way where the track becomes metalled.

5 Stride on for nearly a mile towards Sheader. Cross the Allt Dearg and climb the slope beyond, to where, on the right, a short stretch of access road turns acutely right to a white bungalow. At this junction go through, on the right, a double metal hurdle used as a gate. Walk down the field beside a stream to come to a gate. Beyond, with the stream now to your right, descend the river bank on a

30

Opposite-leaved Golden Saxifrage

little path to cross a footbridge over the River Conon. Climb the banking and walk on over the pasture, keeping to the left of a green barn. Continue on to pass through a gate in the right end of the fence. Stride on up towards the left of a ruined byre to a gate to the road. Walk right to return to the parking area.

Curlew

Practicals

Type of walk. A good walk for a good day. The Trotternish ridge is often clear when mist enshrouds the Cuillin—but do not attempt Ben Edra in the mist. The walk is over tracks, paths, pathless moorland and round grassy slopes. Spectacular views when you achieve the summit. After heavy rain some river crossings will be awkward.

Distance:	8½ miles / 13.5 km
Time:	4–5 hours
Map:	OS Landranger 23

8

Greshornish Point

Park in a small quarry on the left, 2 miles along the minor road, signed Greshornish (and Greshornish Hotel), which leaves, right, the A850 Portree to Dunvegan, 1½ miles west of Edinbane. The quarry lies just before a track on the left and a cottage, grid ref. 338535.

On the walk look for lichens, especially **tree lungwort**, on tree trunks. This is typical of the north and west of Britain and is unable to tolerate pollution. Lichens exist in a variety of colour and form. The body of the plant consists of two

Sea cliffs,
Greshornish Point

different organisms growing intimately together; these are a fungus and an alga. The fungus makes up the bulk of the plant and the algal cells are buried in it. The latter, being green, make the food for the fungus which is colourless and unable to manufacture its food.

As you go look for grassy mounds enriched with otter spraints and keep a vigilant look-out for the **otters**. They belong to the same family as stoat, mink and weasel. They are well equipped for their aquatic life, with short powerful legs, dense waterproof fur, long sturdy tails and webbed feet. They have long sensitive whiskers which help them hunt prey in the dark and in murky waters. They are common around the rocky coasts and can be seen diving for fish at any time of the day. In spite of living in the sea they are river otters; the sea otter lives in the Pacific Ocean and is quite different.

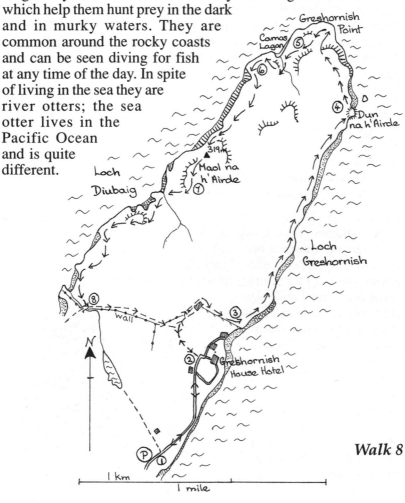

Walk 8

33

1 Walk on along the road from the quarry ignoring two tracks off to the left. Cross an old cattle grid and pass between stone gate posts to follow the road through a delightful deciduous wood, where the tree trunks are green with lichen. Ignore the drive to the right which leads to Greshornish House Hotel and continue straight ahead until the road bends sharply right. There is a 'no parking' sign here.

2 Leave the road, which continues down to a fish farm, and take a metal gate on the left to walk on along a reinforced fenced track. Follow this as it bends right. (The gate on the left is the one you come through on the way back.) A short distance further on the track passes through a gate into the driveway of a cottage. Just before the cottage driveway take a gate in the wall on the left giving access to a grassy track. Follow this to the end of the fence round the cottage, and then turn right and follow a series of indistinct paths down by the fence, and then a wall, to the coast.

3 Turn left, using a path which runs close to the beaches and low cliffs—where there is bracken the path is clear and grassy but in heather the way divides and wanders. Enjoy the views over to Trotternish as you go. Look for oystercatchers, curlews and gulls. After 2km you reach Dun na-h-Airde situated on an isolated stack, with cliffs on three sides and a steep climb up the fourth. The wall is ruined but the entrance is still clear to see.

4 From the dun go on to cross a beach of black basalt pebbles and climb to higher ground. Take the left branch where the path divides. It climbs up across a bog and then contours round the hillside, quite high up. It takes a line through boulders, and then heather, on a wide shelf before coming down to Greshornish Point at the end of the headland. Pause at the point where there are rocks to sit on and some columnar basalt too. Look out to see Eilean Mor, Eilean Beag, Lyndale Point, Trotternish and the Ascrib Islands. Beyond, lies Harris. Here you might see gannets diving close inshore and spot curious common seals and dolphins.

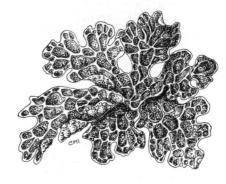

Tree Lungwort

34

5 To continue, take a path at the inland side of a boggy flat area south-west of the point leading to a little hidden bay, Camas Lagan. Cross the burn which runs into the bay and climb up the far side. Turn right to contour under the hilltop. Go on along another wide grassy shelf. Walk to its far end to admire the splendid sea cliffs— the haunt of a sea eagle.

6 From here, turn left to cross the bog behind and begin the climb to Maol na h-Airde, the highest point on the peninsula. The way is drier nearer the cliff edge and the views are stunning but you may prefer to use the sheep tracks further back from the edge. The summit provides a superb view of the entire peninsula.

7 Descend by following a broad sloping shelf west of the summit and then take one of the tracks leading south-west towards the coastline. Go on the undulating way, with good views of cliffs and stacks, and then contour round a bay with a short stack on a grassy pedestal. After a short climb descend towards a burn with a sturdy wall on the far side. Do not cross the burn but follow the path round ahead above it until the path descends to join a grassy track which passes through a gate in the wall on the right. (If you turn right and pass through you come eventually to the head of Loch Diubaig—a grassy isolated spot with a beach of black pebbles and a wide burn.)

8 For this walk turn left. Follow the track, climbing at first, and then descending to pass through a gate into trees. In a short distance you come to the gate noted on the outward journey. Go through and turn right. Follow the reinforced track down to the road behind Greshornish House Hotel, where you turn right to return to the quarry.

Practicals

Type of walk: An excellent walk: the way is quite rough and so it takes longer than you would expect. The east side is pleasant and the dun is dramatically positioned. The west side, with its stupendous cliffs and stacks, makes the walk special.

Distance: 4 miles / 6.5 km
Time: 3 hours
Map: OS Landranger 23

9

Loch Losait, Waternish Forest

Park to the right of the gate at the start of the track to Loch Losait, well clear of the loading bay, grid ref. 263573. This lies opposite to an exit gate from Waternish House on the northern outskirts of Stein. (Make sure you do not block any gate.)

Since the previous edition of this book, the ownership of the **forest** has changed. The author has been told that the new owner does not intend to harvest the trees. Tracks have been sturdily reinforced and some new ones have been put in. At the time of writing the way seems rather bleak and bare but nature will soon start to colonise the sides of the tracks, returning them to their earlier pleasing state.

As you walk through the forest you might disturb a **woodcock**. These birds shun the open by day, crouching quietly in woods, their buff, brown and black plumage and markings make them invisible until disturbed. Then the birds rise with a swish of wings. They dodge through the trees, or across the track, to drop down after a short flight and are lost to sight. On spring evenings they fly over their territory making a strange creaking and whistling noise—this is called 'roding'.

Loch Losait

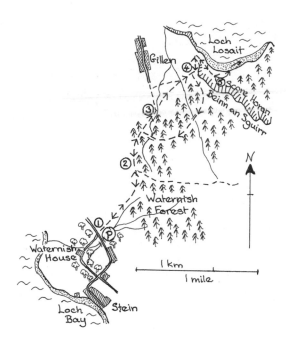

1 With your back to the waters of the Little Minch, go through the gate to walk the sturdily reinforced track, climbing steadily onto open pastures. Pass through the next gate and continue along the way now bordered by conifers on the right. In summer, the wide verge to the left can be a colourful garden of ragwort, heather, hayrattle, kidney vetch, scabious and yarrow, interspersed by lush ferns.

2 Continue on through conifers now on both sides of the track. Ignore the next two right turns. Suddenly, framed by the last of the conifers, you see ahead, Loch Snizort, and the Ascrib Islands seeming to float on the sparkling water. After a mile from the start, go on along the continuing pleasing track, easier underfoot and with a few muddy places. The track takes you out into open pastures, with rows of conifers now far over to the right.

3 Ignore the track to your left, which leads to the settlement of Gillen, its houses scattered along fine cliffs and go on along the track to the top of high cliffs overlooking delightful Loch Losait. Here you might spot the toy-like Lochmaddy–Uig ferry heading for its destination.

37

4 Turn left and begin your descent of the very wide track. Follow round its wide dog-leg turn and descend steeply to the black beach below. Stroll along the shore. Look across the water to see Meall Suiramach, the high point of the Quiraing. The beach has a wide grassy sward, backed by rows of conifers, the haunt of goldcrest, willow warbler and coal tit. Above, the steep slopes are covered with willow, birch, rowan and oak. Higher still rear the castellated and pinnacled tops of Beinn an Sguirr. Look for seals just offshore and, further out, you might spot gannets diving. At the time of writing, sadly the beach has received an enormous amount of litter from the sea.

5 Return up the wide track and at the viewpoint go on ahead. Follow the reinforced track through the plantation and where it swings right. This is where you might disturb a woodcock. The track continues steadily right and, at an open area free of conifers, you can look across the Little Minch to see Harris and Lewis. On joining your outward track, turn left and retrace your steps back to the gate at the start of the walk.

Practicals

Type of walk: Good tracks and fine views. Just the walk for a windy or damp day.

Distance: 4½ miles / 7.2 km
Time: 2–3 hours
Map: OS Landranger 23

Unish and Waternish Point

Park in the large lay-by, grid ref. 224614, opposite Trumpan Church on the most westerly point of the narrow road that runs along the west coast of the Waternish peninsula.

From the windy graveyard of **Trumpan Church** there are fine views over sea and moorland, and down into Ardmore Bay. A gable end and a few crumbling walls is all that is left of the church. One Sabbath day in 1578 a party of MacDonalds from Uist in the

Trumpan Church

Western Isles, seeking revenge for past atrocities, landed in the bay and surprised the local MacLeods at worship. They set fire to the thatch of the church, burning it and all within. A woman sitting on a nearby hillock saw the deed and raced to Dunvegan Castle to raise the alarm. The MacDonalds continued pillaging and burning and when the MacLeods arrived the arsonists raced to their boats in Ardmore Bay. Alas the tide had receded and left them high and dry. They turned to fight the MacLeods but all were slain.

Walk 10

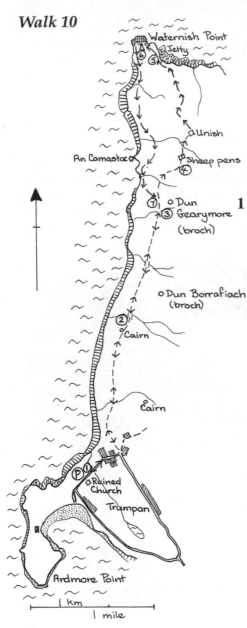

1 Walk left from the parking area, along the straight road, to where it makes a right-angled turn. Here turn left through a gate, with a sign saying 'No dogs'. Follow the track beyond, as it leads out into extensive heather moorland. Pass through the next gate and walk on with the bubbling calls of curlews coming from deeper into the moorland. Look right to see a cairn on a distant hillock, a memorial to John MacLeod of Unish who was killed around 1530 in a battle against the MacDonalds of Trotternish. About a mile from the first gate you come to another cairn, close beside the track. This commemorates Roderick MacLeod, son of John, who was killed in the same battle.

2 Continue on along the track and follow it as it descends a little to pass, on the right, a ruined croft. This lies close to a wide shallow burn that sometimes makes the track very muddy, especially if the cattle have used the track too. On the right and well away from the path, are the bare remains of Dun Borrafiach, a broch which must have given the defenders good views of approaching marauders.

3 Go on along the easy-to-walk track until you see, also to the right, another broch, Dun Gearymore. This is more accessible but little remains of the structure. The rabbits and whinchats do not seem to mind and among the litter of boulders grow ferns and foxgloves. This is also a splendid viewpoint of the moorland around and the extensive seascape. From now on you have several glimpses of the lighthouse on Waternish Point. Stroll the path as it turns slightly east and comes to the ruinous settlement of Bail' an Tailleir (the town of tailors). The foundations of several crofts huddle together close to a pretty burn.

4 Follow the track as it veers left to two gates (which form a sheep pen). Pass through and strike across the field towards the large ruin of Unish House. Go through a gate and step across a stream. Close by the house are the remains of more buildings and behind it is a large walled field. Step across the next fence and walk left, heading for Waternish Point. Use sheep trods to carry on over the glorious turf and keep to higher ground to your right as you continue. Look here for golden plovers. Wind right round the next hillock, cross a little burn and walk its grassy side to the shore line.

5 Bear left in the direction of the unmanned lighthouse, pausing as you go to view Duntulm and the Trotternish Ridge. Look down on the little natural harbour and a jetty with a ramp. Look also for seals and the dramatic cliffs. Follow the grassy way, partly edged with white-lichened rocks, from the ramp to reach the lighthouse, painted white and with a bright green door. From here there are great views to the Western Isles.

6 Beyond the lighthouse, clear marks made by the wheels of a tractor lead you on. Follow these tracks faithfully, over the short cropped turf, along the stunning coastline. They take you safely round the geos where you might see splendid stacks just offshore. Keep with the tracks to pass through a gate in a fence. Beyond, continue on sheep tracks, which eventually bring you to a ruined wall. Pass through, cross a burn and follow along the inside of a derelict fence,

Golden Plover

with the cliffs beyond. Then head inland following a clear trod up the left side of a turf dyke. Follow this, still inland, across two pastures to rejoin your outward route, close to Dun Gearymore Broch.

7 Turn right to follow the track back to the gate to the road. Turn right for the parking area by the church.

Practicals

Type of walk: A splendid walk through moorland and then on over delightful turf to Waternish Point. The area around the settlement must have been difficult to leave when the area was 'cleared' The villagers had a stream, good pastures for their sheep, access to the sea, a place to land their catch and a quiet secluded site to lead a tranquil life.

Distance: 8 miles / 12.8 km
Time: 4–5 hours
Map: OS Landranger 23

11

Coral Beaches

Park in the car park, grid ref. 233537, reached by a minor road running north from Dunvegan to the small township of Claigan. The car park lies to the left of a right angled bend. There is a sign saying 'No dogs'.

The **'coral'** is *Lithothamnion calcareum,* which grows unattached or occasionally encrusting pebbles on the extreme lower shore and in shallow water. It is a red seaweed which lays down an exoskeleton of chalk, not a coral at all. When alive it is violet-pink in colour, but becomes bleached white when dead.

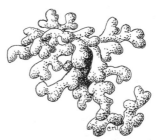

Lithothamnion 'coral'

Coral Beach

Walk 11

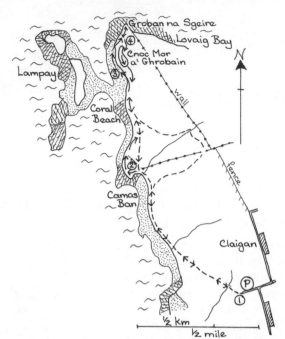

1 Leave the car park by a kissing gate at the far end. Follow the good stony track that takes you across a burn and goes down through a field to the shore, where it continues along the back of the beach. Walk on to Camas Ban, the first coral beach. If the tide is in there is very little coral visible.

2 To continue you have a choice; either to walk inland and go through a gap broken in the impressive wall and up the well used path beyond or, more interestingly, potter on around the headland and round the end of the wall. From here there are excellent views of the second coral beach, which is really golden, making a pleasant change on an island where most beaches are black. The beach is backed by machair and a delightful conical hill, Cnoc Mor a'Ghrobain. The tidal islet of Lampay lies offshore.

3 Follow a path round below the hill to the headland, Groban na Sgeire, where there are remains of a small earthwork and much basalt. Look for otter spraints and places where they have rolled. Enjoy the view of the island of Isay offshore. This is as far as you can walk, progress being impeded by a large wall with all the gaps fenced with barbed wire.

4 Return across the grass behind the headland and wind up onto the hill, which has a longish ridge projecting towards you. Follow the ridge to the top to enjoy the splendid view of the islands of Isay, Mingay and Clett, with Ardmore Point behind. To the west you can see the cliffs up to Dunvegan Head. In the distance the misty smudge is Harris. Look for wheatears flitting about the outcrops. Come straight down the front of the hill to the beach or circle round behind for a more gentle descent. Go back along your outward path.

Wheatear

Milkwort

Practicals

Type of walk: Very pleasant and easy, which can be enjoyed by small children and their parents. Take your waterproofs and perhaps a beach mat on which to sunbathe—the coral is very hard. The best beach is almost at the headland, so make sure you walk far enough.

Distance: 4 miles / 6.5 km
Time: 3 hours
Map: OS Landranger 23

12

Healabhal Mhor—Macleod's Table, North

Park in one of several lay-bys close to the start of the track to ruined Osdale, grid ref. 243464. These are reached by turning off the A863 at Lonmore. Follow the B884 as it comes close to an inlet of Loch Dunvegan. From here both MacLeod's Tables can be seen.

Healabhal Mhor (1,539ft/469m) has a larger 'table' than Healabhal Bheag (1,605ft/489m) (MacLeod's Table south) but, of the two, the southern table is the higher. Legend says that these strange flat-topped hills were chopped off to make a bed and a table for St Columba when he was refused accommodation by a local chieftain. In fact geologists suggest they are flat as a result of weathering of the basalt lava, which has been laid down in horizontal planes.

Another **legend** of the tables is about MacLeod, the ninth chief. Lofty lords at the King's Court in Edinburgh made derogatory remarks about his table in Skye. MacLeod responded by inviting them to the island for a meal. He took them on to the summit (the largest of tables) for a great banquet, illuminated by MacLeod's clansmen holding flaming torches (the most candelabra), with the star-studded sky above (for the roof of his great 'mansion'). The

Macleod's Tables

story has it that the lofty lords were suitably impressed—it would have been dangerous not to be, with all Macleod's clansmen standing around.

Walk 12

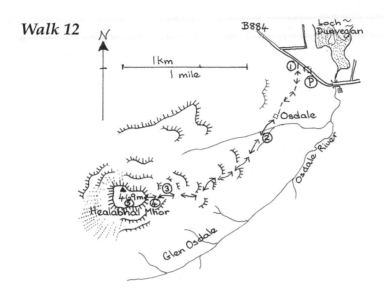

1 Close to the parking area look for a gate to a track on the west side of the road. Walk the track towards two ruined buildings, all that remains of the settlement of Osdale. The way rapidly deteriorates into a sketchy path. Go through a gap in the fence and continue down to a tree-lined burn, a tributary of the Osdale River. Generally this can be crossed on convenient stones.

2 Follow sheep tracks that lead from the pretty burn and continue across heather moorland where you might spot a short-eared owl quartering the ground for voles. Make your way, steadily west, in the direction of the summit. On reaching the base of a fairly sharp heather-clad slope look for the easiest way up and then go on to climb the rougher but less steep ground above. From here enjoy the views of Dunvegan Castle on the other side of its loch. To the left you can see the 'seal islands' and further along the shore the coral beach, which appears pale lemon if the sun is shining. Beyond lie the islands off Waternish, with Ardmore Point and Waternish Point in the distance. Out to sea the hills of the distant Hebrides are seen strung along the horizon.

3 Continue climbing upwards, finding the best way round the rocky outcrops and ridges of rock, keeping your eye on the summit for as long as it is visible. Pause regularly to look down on Loch Bracadale and its many islands. Over to the far left you might be rewarded with a glimpse of the Cuillin.

4 Then the steep climb to the Table lies ahead. Keep well to the left away from the edge of the cliffs that drop sheer. Suddenly the flat top lies at your feet. Stroll across the mossy plateau to the far side, keeping to the left of a lochan. Look for club-mosses growing among the moss. To the left lies Healabhal Bheag (MacLeod's Table South), a mountain with steep sides and jagged slopes. Beyond the tops of the two giants, the Tables, the sea sparkles and you might spot the Cuillin on Rum.

5 Return across the Table and look for the ruined crofts far below. When you have your bearings, begin your descent.

Short-eared owl

Practicals

Type of walk: Steepish ascents (and descents) over heather moorland and bands of rock. Pleasing views as you climb the pathless way.

Distance: 4½ miles / 7 km
Time: 4 hours
Map: OS Landranger 23

Waterstein Head

You may wish to complete a second walk to Neist Point after climbing Waterstein Head; see 13 b.

Park in a large space above Loch Mor, before reaching the scattered houses of Waterstein, on the left of the road, grid ref. 148488. This is reached by taking the B884 through Glendale. Continue on for just over a mile to take a narrow road, on the left, signed Waterstein and Neist Point.

Waterstein Head is one of Skye's most stunning cliffs. Sheep graze on its very edge and sometimes below the edge; dogs are not allowed on the Head for obvious reasons. The turf of the hill is full of rabbit holes and in autumn there is a huge variety of wax cap fungi, ranging from bright scarlet through lemon-yellow to white. Look for buzzards hovering in the updraught above the cliff edge and ravens performing aerobatics, closing their wings and rolling over.

The **views** from the Head are splendid, with Neist Point and its lighthouse below, and beyond it the Western Isles—South Uist's Beinn More and Hecla appear directly opposite. To the north there are exciting cliffs ending in Sky Cliff (Biod nan Athair). South lies the great sweep of Moonen Bay, with two cliff waterfalls, Ramasaig Cliff and finally the Hoe.

Wax Caps

49

1 Take the path leading away from the car park along the escarpment edge, following beside an old dyke (wall). This gives easy walking across the hillside, climbing gently, with lovely views over Loch Mor. Cross a derelict fence. Look for the gap in the far bank of a small ravine and opposite to it, descend to cross the burn in the bottom. Go through the gap.

2 Continue to follow the dyke as it climbs the hillside—it makes a sweep round to the left which you can avoid by walking straight across, parallel with the escarpment edge. The turf is short and makes for easy walking. At the top of this ascent Waterstein Head proper comes into view, with its steep prow towering above. Go on along the short grass near the edge of the cliff, which becomes steeper and rockier.

3 Step over the derelict fence, which appears on your left and walk along inside it. Follow the fence, now renewed, where it turns to the right with the turn of the cliff.

4 Go on inside the fence up the steep grassy field and across to the top corner of the fence, where there is a trig point. The views are magnificent as they have been all the way up.

5 Return by your outward route.

Practicals

Type of walk: A really pleasing walk on short grass, with amazing views to encourage you to the summit.

Distance:	2½ miles / 4 km
Time:	2 hours
Map:	OS Landranger 23
NB:	Do not attempt in the mist or on a very windy day.

---

13 b

Neist Point and the Lighthouse

Park in the lighthouse car park, grid ref. 132478. This is reached by continuing on the B884 beyond the car park used for the walk to Waterstein Head (13 a).

Look for a **colony of shags** sitting on rocks at the foot of the cliffs. For the first six or seven months of the year the shag has a resplendent conspicuous recurved crest. It feeds on fish captured at speed under water. Sometimes it nests on ledges but generally it chooses a wave-washed cave and sits on a nest of rotting malodorous seaweed.

1 Walk out of the far end of the car park along a concrete path and follow it where it turns left before descending steeply by steps and a slope. Look left to see the huge hoist used to winch goods down the cliffs.

Neist Point (from Waterstein Head)

The path crosses the hoist at ι
bottom and you are asked not to u
the path whilst the hoist is working

2 Follow the path as it crosses a wide
grassy plateau. It then ascends to
hug the edge of a hill from where
you have a grand view of
Waterstein Head (walk 13 a).
Beyond, the path slopes downhill
to cross a largish grassy area where
once the lighthouse keepers played
golf. The way then leads to the
lighthouse. It is no longer manned
and some of the complex of
buildings have been turned into
holiday cottages. In summer there
is a snack bar.

3 Go left round the enclosure fence—here you might just spot a stoat
carrying prey under it. Go on to visit the small jetty and its nearby
rock pools where turnstones poke about in the water. Then continue
to the Point to watch gannets diving out at sea and enjoy the amazing
views of Waterstein Head 'front-on'.

4 Return by your outward route, perhaps walking along the cliff top
for a short way to obtain good views back to the lighthouse.

Practicals

Type of walk: A short walk for spectacular views of the cliff-girt most westerly point of Skye. Don't forget your waterproofs because some of Skye's worst gales occur here.

Distance:	1 mile / 1.5 km
Time:	1 hour
Map:	OS Landranger 23

...asaig, Lorgill and the Hoe

Parking. Drive the B884 from Lonmore, south of Dunvegan, to Glendale. One mile beyond, take a minor road on the left, signed Ramasaig. Follow it for about 4 miles over the moors to its end. At the time of writing, there is parking at the road end for 4–5 cars, grid ref. 164443. This is the best place. Or go through the gate and park, grid ref. 165441, on a large area by some animal pens, taking care not to cause obstruction. Alternatively, two passing places further back up the road there is a flat area opposite the passing place which could be used.

Lorgill was once a thriving community with a dozen or more families. In 1830, at very short notice, they were ordered to leave to make way for tenant farmers and their sheep. With the threat of imprisonment for failing to do so, they had to board a ship at Loch Snizort bound for Nova Scotia, as part of the notorious Clearances.

Look for **fulmars** around the headland of Hoe Rape. In winter they are oceanic wanderers. In summer they nest in large numbers

Waterstein and Ramasaig Heads from the Hoe

Fulmar

on cliff ledges. They are recognised by their grey back, white head, tubular nostril and their stiff flight on outstretched wings, which are as steady as the wings of a glider. When nesting they can be aggressive and when disturbed spit a foul fishy liquid—be warned.

Walk 14

1 Go through the gate at the end of the road and walk past farm buildings and animal pens to another gate beside a barn. Beyond, go on the stony track (called Lon Ban) leading to another gate and then out onto the moor, where the path winds round, climbing gently, passing an old croft and lots of old lazy beds. Watch out for a golden eagle that quarters this area. Continue to the summit of the pass from where you will want to pause to enjoy the views of MacLeod's Tables.

2 As the track begins to descend, look left to see a fine waterfall on the Lorgill Burn. Go through a stout new fence and head on down to Lorgill, zig-zagging gently down over sheep-cropped pastures towards a building by the river. Go through two gates in quick succession beside this building. Do not attempt to cross the river, but turn right on its bank. Ford a small burn and then follow the river down to the shore. The walking is very pleasant, over short turf passing, as you go, scattered ruined crofts and old cultivation

Harebells

ridges. The beach is spectacular, backed by dark cliffs, with views to the Western Isles.

3 Leave the beach and climb steeply, over grass, to a ruined intake wall (dyke). Then zig-zag up to join a path (seen clearly from below) which makes a rising traverse across the face of the hillside.

4 Continue west, along the cliff edge, using sheep tracks as near or as far back as you are happy. Pause often to enjoy the magnificent views. Then go on along the cliff edge or, head inland towards higher ground where the going is easier on the edge of a small basalt escarpment. (If you keep to the cliff edge you will come to a ruined fence which you follow inland.) Head for the summit of the Hoe (133m) and enjoy the views of MacLeod's Tables and the distant Cuillin.

5 Go on along sheep tracks, northwards, soon to reach short turf above the cliff edge, where you continue onwards to the headland of Gob na Hoe. This sticks out dramatically with a drop of 200m to the sea, and beyond it is the ring of cliffs around Moonen Bay, ending in the lighthouse at Neist Point. Go on and descend gently over the pleasing turf, avoiding the more heathery and boggy slopes inland, to the headland of Hoe Rape, another good viewpoint and where many fulmars nest. Continue on the delightful descent to reach the lands once cultivated by the people of Ramasaig before the Clearances.

6 Head inland towards the distant wood at the road end close to your parking area. Ford the burn, Abhainn an Loin Bhain. If it is in

spate you may have to wade or go down to the beach to cross easily on the pebbles—though this involves negotiating a loose wet gully back up the low cliff.

Otter

7 A track beyond the ford leads through a gate into a grassy pasture full of stone heaps and signs of former cultivation. Follow an old path above a line of stones and ford a small burn. Then head directly uphill, with a fence to your right, soon to join a tractor track which brings you out by the barn on the original stony track (Lon Ban). Turn left to go through the gate to return to your car.

Practicals

Type of walk: This is a delightful circular walk, with superb views. The cliff top requires care and should be avoided in windy conditions.

Distance:	5 miles / 8 km
Time:	3–4 hours
Map:	OS Landranger 23
NB:	Dogs are not allowed on the Hoe.

15

Healabhal Bheag (MacLeod's Table South)

Take the A863 south from Dunvegan and, after a mile, turn left at Lonmore onto the B884, signed Glendale. After ½ mile/1km turn left, signed Orbost. Park in a large space on the road corner before Orbost House, grid ref. 256434.

Healabhal Bheag, 1,601ft/488m, (bheag meaning little) is higher than Healabhal Mhor, 1,538ft/469m, (mhor meaning big) but the summit plateau of the latter is larger, giving it its appellation.

A large board at the parking area welcomes visitors to explore the **Orbost Estate**. It asks that all gates are closed and that dogs should be kept on leads when livestock are present. It also asks that vehicles are parked without obstructing roadways, other vehicles or the steading entrance. It states that the track to the beach is for walkers only and is not suitable for most vehicles.

The board continues: 'Orbost Estate was purchased by Highlands and Islands Enterprise in 1997 in order to provide opportunities

Loch Bharcasaig

for sustainable rural development in this corner of north west Skye. Planned developments include new smallholdings and associated housing for families, commercial and amenity woodlands and organic agriculture'.

Walk 15

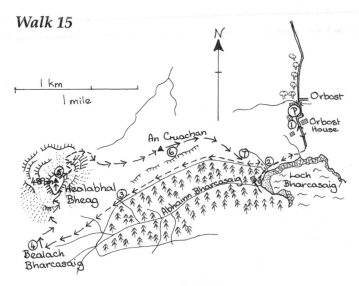

1 Take the track that winds past Orbost House. Follow it as it turns right to run above the shore of Bharcasaig Bay. Pause here to enjoy the views of the Cuillin, the cliffs north of Talisker, Rum and Canna. Notice the natural arch on the corner of the left of the bay. Stand here quietly and you might spot an otter running between the rocks and into the water. Continue until the track crosses a burn lined with hazels.

2 Then, immediately, take on the right, a small path between the burn and the fence at the beginning of a larch plantation. The way is quite steep but delightful—a secret path under hazels. Soon the larch gives way to pine. Turn left at the fence corner and follow, for about 1¼ miles/2km, a terraced path that keeps above the forest. It crosses old cultivation ridges and passes the remains of a turf and stone dyke (wall). You are very sheltered here—the hillside goes up steeply on the right and the forest protects you to the left.

3 Cross a burn on slippery rocks and then another. Where the fence turns away left and descends sharply, leave it to go on ahead and slightly uphill. Follow the now indistinct path as it passes through

59

an area of small grassy mounds—probably the remains of shielings. Continue on, heading right and keeping to higher ground, to avoid the worst of the bog, to come to the Bealach (pass) Bharcasaig. On the bealach itself the path crosses an indistinct dyke, the crossing marked by a heap of stones, white with lichen.

4 From this mound head, right, up a grassy ravine to another turf and stone dyke. Follow the top of this dyke steeply up to the right as it ascends towards Healabhal Bheag. At the foot of a small crag follow the dyke round to the right, then leave it to go up through a break in the crag. Cross the flattish area beyond and then begin to climb steeply over close-cropped grass and heather. Zigzag up on sheep tracks, picking

Golden Eagles

C.M.Isherwood

60

the easiest line through small crags. Join a more defined path, which still zig-zags, until, just below the rocks of the summit, it heads off right. Follow it round and up through a break in the crags onto the summit plateau. The latter is flat, with a grassy hump at the south-west end, a walled trig point in the middle and a small shelter at the east end. The view is stunning. Look for all the Western Isles, the Shiants, Trotternish, the mainland, the Cuillin, Rum and Canna. Here also you might see a golden eagle and a flock of golden plover.

5 Walk over to the small stone shelter, then beyond it to a cairn which marks the start of the path down. This goes along a short narrow ridge ending in a hump with a great prow of cliff. Before you reach this end, turn off left and make your way down carefully over the steep grass and scree, following a clear narrow, stony path. It curves round to the right as the slope eases, until you are directly below the dramatic rocky prow which soars above. The grassy slope continues less steeply and the walking is very pleasant. Descend to an area of rocky knolls beyond which the spur continues but becomes very wide and boggy on top. Choose one of the faint paths and keep as far as possible to the higher ground avoiding the worst of the bogs. Head for An Cruachan, a rocky knoll, and the highest point on the spur.

6 Then go down to the right, keeping above the crags and taking advantage of the drier ground on the slope. Head for Orbost. Once directly above the ruined turf dyke, crossed near the beginning of the walk, descend quite easily over the steep grassy and heathery slopes to join the dyke. Cross it to follow the outward path to the top corner of the wood. Return down the hidden path beside the burn and retrace your steps along the track to Orbost.

Practicals

Type of walk: A challenging exciting hill walk, though not all on paths and quite steep in places. Some of the going is rather wet.

Distance:	5 miles / 8 km
Time:	3–4 hours
Map:	OS Landranger 23

16

MacLeod's Maidens

Take the A863 south from Dunvegan and, after a mile, turn left at Lonmore onto the B884, signed Glendale. After ½ mile turn left, signed Orbost. Park in a large space on the road corner before Orbost House, grid ref. 256434.

MacLeod's Maidens are three sea stacks, the finest of the many seen along this most impressive stretch of coastline, where there are also dramatic natural arches and caves. The tallest stack, known as the Mother (208ft high), lies nearest to the cliff edge. Beyond, stand her two daughters—one tall and thin and the other round and dumpy, sitting on a plinth of rock. Some say that from a certain angle the mother appears to be nodding to her daughters. Legend relates that the stacks are the wife and two daughters of the Fourth Chief of the Clan MacLeod who drifted in their boat before a strong westerly wind and were shipwrecked here off Idrigill Point.

MacLeod's Maidens

1 Walk down the forestry track towards Loch Bharcasaig, where the waves come in over black sand and pebbles and where you might see common seals and otters. Cross Abhainn Bharcasaig by its bridge and follow the way as it begins to climb, with conifers to the right and splendid views across the loch to the left.

2 Go on along the track into the forest. The sea views are gone but ahead you might just glimpse the summit of Beinn na Boineid, rearing into the sky. After a short descent the track brings you to Forse Burn, which you cross. Go on uphill through the immature plantings which will soon obscure more of the glorious views. Continue on the track, now diminished to a cairned path, which climbs steadily to a cairned pass, with Beinn na Moine on the sea side.

3 Descend steadily to cross the slopes above Brandarsaig Bay by keeping above the fence and crossing it a couple of times. Continue on to a sheepfold and

Walk 16

Otter

63

cross a burn to climb the path beyond. Carry on to a gate to emerge from the young forest.

4 Press on along the path to where it passes through a short heather-clad narrow glen between the low hills of Steineval and Ard Bheag. Pause here to climb to the ridge of Ard Bheag for a fine view of two unusual natural arches in Camas na h-Uamha—the strand of the cave. Return to the path and continue on. To the left lie the cliffs of Idrigill Point.

5 From now on there are no more cairns and the path becomes indistinct. The way keeps above a greensward and passes between knolls and there are many sheep trods. A cairn away to the left marks the cliff edge and you should approach this with great care to look down on the unexpected magnificent Maidens far below, where great white-topped breakers crash around the stacks. Walk on to the next bay for an excellent and often less windy view of the Maidens.

6 Your return is by your outward route.

Practicals

Type of walk: An exciting walk to the dramatic coastline of Duirinish. There is a path of sorts all the way but it is a strenuous walk. Choose a good day and allow yourself plenty of time.

Distance: 10 miles / 16 km
Time: 5–6 hours
Map: OS Landranger 23

Dun Beag and Oronsay

Park in the good car park, with picnic tables, off the A863, opposite to the entrance to the broch, grid ref. 337385.

Dun Beag Broch (little fort) is a defensive tower that dates from the Iron Age. It stands high on its hill overlooking Loch Bracadale, with much of its stonework intact. It is believed to have been built by farmers and herdsmen, perhaps between 400 BC and 200 BC. From then on, at various times and at least until the late Middle Ages, it was used as a refuge against attack or in times of danger. The broch was excavated between 1914 and 1920 and many treasures were found including spears, knives for hunting and fighting, crucible and ingot moulds for bronze working, an antler pick for digging, a stone lamp, coins and some personal ornaments made of stone, bone, bronze, gold and glass.

Oronsay, Norse for ebb-tide island, is cut off from the shore at high tide. It is reached by a 200m long pebble causeway. The walk to the island should be completed when the tide is on the ebb and then you will have no anxiety about having to wait for several hours for the causeway to reappear!

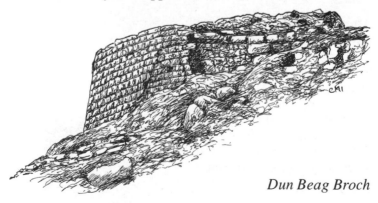

Dun Beag Broch

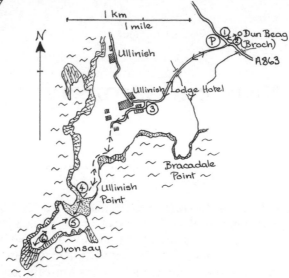

1 From the parking area cross the road, pass through a kissing gate and take the path which leads through heather and bracken to the dun.

2 Return from the broch and turn left. After a short distance go right down a minor road, signed 'Ullinish' There is a fine view of MacLeod's Tables to the right and the Cuillin to the left, with Ardtreck lighthouse and the cottages of Portnalong in front.

3 After 1 mile/1.5 km take a turning on the left and follow it along to the road end, where there is a sharp left turn and then the entrance to a cottage. To the right of the cottage, climb the stile and continue along a track to a second gate. Beyond, the track goes round a tiny bay to finish in some boggy ground.

Gannet

4 Go through the next gate in a fence from where there is a great view of Oronsay ahead. Descend a rocky gully to the causeway and cross to a sandy beach on the island.

5 Now you can begin your exploration of the fine little wedge-shaped island which tilts so dramatically, downwards towards Ullinish. There are no paths but make full use of sheep tracks up the dry, grassy, steepish slope to come, suddenly, to the cliff edge—be warned. Take care as you stand to enjoy the magnificent view over Loch Bracadale, with superb views of the Talisker cliffs and those of Fiskavaig, and of the island of Wiay. Look out towards the horizon for splashes made by gannets and terns as they plunge headlong after fish. Keep an eye on the tide!

6 When you have enjoyed the utter peace found here, return by the same route.

Terns

Practicals

Type of walk: Dun Beag, with its 13 ft thick circular wall, long narrow entrance, remains of a stone staircase and guard cell is an exciting place to visit especially for youngsters. The walk out to Oronsay, to be attempted on an ebb tide only, is equally exciting and if the sun is setting a particularly lovely trip.

Distance: 3 miles / 5 km
Time: 1–2 hours
Map: OS Landranger 23

18

Talisker and Fiskavaig

Park just before Talisker House, grid ref. 326306. Talisker lies at the end of the road at the west end of Gleann Oraid.

Along the route on your 'there and back' walk, look for **hard fern** growing in the banks of the track, with the barren fronds prostrate on the ground and the fertile ones springing up from the same clump. Heath and heather flower along the edges too. On the open moor meadow pipits and wheatears abound. Watch for stonechats and whinchats sitting atop heather shoots. Cotton grass flourishes in the many wet areas and lousewort in the ditches beside the track.

Preshal More and Talisker House

The path from the shore returns through **reed beds** (Phragmites communis), which stretch away on either side and play host to reed buntings and sedge warblers. Overall towers the great prow of Preshal More. Look above the summit for eagles, sometimes harried by ravens and at other times, when an immature bird settles on a rock, by sheep!

Walk 18

▲ 253m

1 Km
1 mile

N

Fiskavaig

Broch

③

Huisgill Burn

②

←Waterfall

▲163m

① R. Talisker

P

⑤

Waterfall

Talisker
Bay

Sleadale
Burn

④

Talisker

Preshal
More
▲317m

Talisker Point o

1 From the car park, walk north on the path across the valley. Go through the farm to a bungalow. By the gate of this dwelling is a sign 'path' with an arrow pointing left. Follow this, go through a gate and walk round the fence of the bungalow until you meet the path coming out at the back of the dwelling's land. Turn left on this lovely track as it zig-zags up the hillside, beside the spectacular waterfall on the Huisgill Burn. This plummets through the heather-clad slopes of a dramatic ravine.

2 Go on up the steep slope and then on less steeply up the valley of the Huisgill Burn. Over the moorland the track deteriorates to a path and becomes indistinct in places, but then the track reappears and you can stride on to the hairpin bend on the Fiskavaig road.

Whinchat

3 This is the point where you make your return, with all the glorious views ahead. At the foot of the fall on the Huisgill Burn is a sun-filled grassy hollow—just the place for a picnic before returning once more to Talisker (now a hotel), where you have parked.

4 Follow the track, straight ahead, signed 'To the Beach'. Go through a kissing gate, which you are asked to close, then walk behind the hotel and cross the Sleadale Burn on a wide bridge. Carry on along the track, through another gate and along the side of the hill. The valley below is a flowery marsh. Near the end of the track there is a spring on the left labelled 'The Piper's Well'. Go through another gate and down to the splendid bay. It is ringed with cliffs, over one of which tumbles a fine waterfall. To the left is a dramatic double stack. Great breakers surge into the bay and crash onto the pebbles in showers of spray.

5 Carry on along the bank behind the bay, until you come to where the Talisker river enters the bay. Here a small muddy path leads inland. At first it is quite wet but soon it crosses a bridge over a ditch and then runs along the bank between the river and the ditch and becomes much drier and quite delightful. In front is the fantastic bulk of Preshal More, dominating the view. In summer the banks of the river are lined with colourful flowers. Then the trees begin, mostly larch with some sycamore and rowan. At first they are bonsaied by the wind, but get bigger further inland. Continue up the bank of the river through the trees and go through a metal gate. The path then continues through the reed bed where, although wet, it is properly made and easily followed, and joins the outward track past the hotel.

Practicals

Type of walk: The first part of this walk is a 'there and back', taking you beside a glorious waterfall. Then the way continues across wild moorland to the road at Fiskavaig. The return is along the same route, with spectacular views ahead as you go. This is followed by a short circular walk to Talisker Bay, a lovely corner of Minginish.

Distance: 5½ miles / 9 km
Time: 3 hours
Map: OS Landranger 32

Glen Eynort and An Cruachan

Leave Carbost by the minor road for Eynort. As you reach the settlement, turn left and park at the side of the road beyond the metal bridge and before the cattle grid into the forest. If this is full go back to the minor road where there is another cattle grid with a huge amount of space, grid ref. 384271.

The Cuillin from above the Bealach Brittle

Compartments of trees in **Glen Brittle Forest** are being harvested as part of the forest plan, the timber going to local sawmills. The compartments will then be replanted to give much greater diversity, with native broadleaves as well as conifers and not as previously in even-aged stands. As you climb at the start of the walk look for Sitka spruce, larch, rowan, sycamore, birch, alder, willow and beech and some unusual trees such as southern beech and two species of eucalyptus. Through the trees flit mixed flocks of small birds including coal and great tits, goldcrests and numerous robins.

1 Cross the cattle grid and continue along the tarmac road into the forest. Almost immediately turn left through a metal barrier and climb gently up the hillside. At the first hairpin bend go right, ignoring the track straight ahead. A clearing in the trees gives a view out over the small community of Eynort with its forestry houses. Along the hill behind the cottages you can see traces of rig and furrow of much earlier cultivation. Above lies horizontally layered basalt. Cross the Allt Daidh and its delightful waterfall on a concrete bridge. The track then makes another hairpin bend and crosses the burn again, where you can see more superb waterfalls.

2 Walk the next hairpin that bears to the right. At another that swings to the left, leave the main track to walk straight ahead. Cross the Allt Daidh for the third time. At the next junction turn right, keeping to the Loch Eynort side of the hill. From here the forest is more open and there are good views down the loch and out to the island of Canna. Below is a ruined church and graveyard and the delightful headland of Faolainn. Continue on a mossy terraced way that descends gently. As you progress the Western Isles come into view.

3 After about 2.5km follow the track as it swings left towards the Bealach Brittle—the Cuillin ridge is suddenly before you. At the T-junction, turn left and follow the track as it winds through mature forest; at the time of writing it is in the process of being felled. Continue uphill through tall conifers to emerge onto the Bealach Brittle and another dramatic view.

72

4 Leave the track by heading off right across a mercifully short stretch of heather and purple moor grass, aiming for a gate in a fence which gives access to the open hill. Turn right beyond to follow a stony track alongside the fence. Follow the track until it diverges from the fence, on the Loch Eynort side of the hill, and peters out on the steep hillside.

5 Zig-zag up the short dry grass until you reach the ridge and continue on up it, walking the short sheep-cropped turf. Use the faint animal tracks along the edge of the escarpment and then climb steeply to the small summit plateau of An Cruachan, with a trig point on its own little crag at the far end. Keep a watchful eye here for golden eagles as you enjoy the stunning panorama. You might also spot a hen harrier circling over the forest below.

6 Retrace your steps from here to the Bealach Brittle and turn left to continue down the forest track, ignoring a turn to the left and then one to the right (the one you came on), until you reach the track that curves right above the shore of Loch Eynort.

7 Walk through the tall trees from where you can see the loch and its fishing boats. Listen for the haunting calls of curlew. Eventually you come to a gate by the cottages at Grula. Go on along the continuing road, past another fine waterfall on the Allt Daidh, to return to the parking area.

Hen Harrier

Practicals

Type of walk: This good circular walk takes you, at first, through Glen Brittle Forest and is ideal if the day is exceedingly windy. It continues up onto An Cruachan adding more challenge to the walk, with the reward of incredible views of the Cuillin and perhaps sightings of golden eagles.

Distance: 10 miles / 16 km
Time: 5–6 hours
Map: OS Landranger 32

20

Glen Brittle to Loch na h-Airde

Park at Glen Brittle campsite, grid ref. 414204.

Loch na h-Airde, a few feet above sea level, has a small man-made channel between it and the sea suggesting that the lovely pool may once have been used as a safe anchorage. It is an idyllic loch where great reed colonises the edges and where herons and water fowl are frequent visitors. To the north of the loch lies a chambered cairn, a stone burial vault, dating from Neolithic times. It was excavated in 1932 and human remains were found. Near the shore is a fortified dwelling place, a dun, with a 4,000 year-old wall close to a sea cliff. The dun was used by families who cultivated the nearby open pastures, farming up until the nineteenth century. Just back from the shore is a ruined house, Rhundunan. Here lived the MacAskills who farmed the land and kept a look-out for the MacLeods.

Rubh' an Dunain

1 Walk through the camp site and climb the stile behind the toilet block. Turn right and follow a footpath that keeps Loch Brittle in sight for all its length. In the first mile, three burns race pell-mell over the moorland, across the path and down the slopes to the sea. When in spate they make spectacular descents over the cliffs that can be seen from the path. The third burn, the Allt Coire Lagan, is too difficult to boulder-hop or wade and you should turn upstream to a wooden bridge, hidden from the path by banks of heather.

2 Beyond the bridge, stroll steadily upwards to join a wider track (it too fords the burn and if you return this way, you will need to use the footbridge—lower down). Where the track diminishes

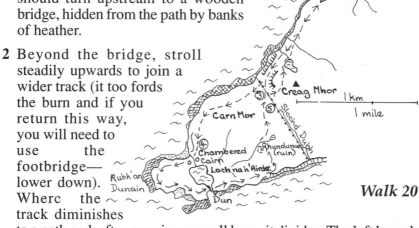

Walk 20

to a path and, after crossing a small burn, it divides. The left branch makes its way inland past a small lochan and climbs Creag Mhor from where there are magnificent views over to Soay, Canna and Rum. The right branch continues above the cliffs. Eventually both paths join. Choose one route on the way out and return by the other.

3 Go on ahead towards a long wall which crosses Slochd Dubh, a wide trough that cuts right across the headland. Pass through a gap in the wall and continue on the path to the top of Carn Mor to enjoy more fabulous views. Look down on Loch na h-Airde. Go on along the path in the direction of a small bay. From this bay a wall runs to the loch. Follow the wall south. Just before the lovely inlet you reach the chambered cairn. About it are the ruins of old croft-houses.

Heron

4 Walk on round the low cliffs of Rubh' an Dunain, with superb views all the way. Cross the rocks blocking the once navigable channel into Loch na h-Airde. Continue on to ascend a promontory where you can explore the dun. Then go on along the cliffs for about half a mile, before beginning to turn away from the sea and walk inland over the heather until eventually you come parallel with the ruinous wall cutting across Slochd Dubh. Continue on avoiding the boggy areas as best you can until you come to the gap passed through on your outward journey.

5 Return from here by the same route (or use the two slight diversions), with the distant Cuillin to encourage you.

Practicals

Type of walk: This is a delightful but strenuous 8½ mile walk with a good path until you reach the headland. Here the terrain can be confusing but fascinating to explore. Choose a good day and allow plenty of time.

Distance: 8½ miles / 13 km
Time: 4–5 hours
Map: OS Landranger 32

21

Coir' a' Ghrunnda from Glen Brittle

Park in the large lay-by before the campsite at Glen Brittle, grid ref. 414205

It is a hard, challenging 3½ miles to **Coir' a' Ghrunnda**, (2,300ft/700m) but the ultimate reward is a loch in a magnificent setting—a wild remote corrie. The water of the pool is a glorious turquoise, the view out to sea superb. Idyllic, yes, but to reach this huge high-sided amphitheatre, a fine glaciated basin, you must be prepared, and able, to walk over rough scree, scramble through a rock field and climb two great bands of slabs.

Loch Coir' a' Ghrunnda

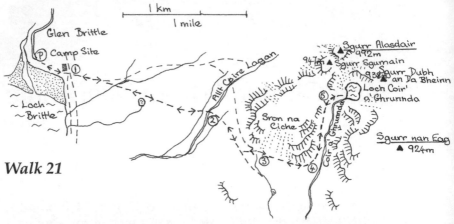

Walk 21

At **Glen Brittle**, near the parking area, enjoy the haymeadows full of summer flowers and various species of grass. As you climb towards the entrance to the corrie look beside the path for heather, hard fern, tormentil, foxgloves, eye bright and scabious. Watch for golden eagles sailing overhead before they glide off out to sea. As you continue upwards notice great patches of alpine lady's mantle, bilberry laden with purple fruit, stone bramble and sweet smelling wild thyme.

1 From Glen Brittle campsite cross the stile behind the public toilets. Walk straight ahead, cross the farm track and keep on up the steep moorland slope, following the track to where it divides. Here take the right branch and continue to a stream, easily crossed on rocks. Walk on along the track, passing a small lochan on the right.

2 Continue on for 4/5 of a mile. At the Allt Coire Lagan, cross the turbulent burn, with care, by numerous well placed boulders. Follow the path beyond and aim for a conspicuously perched boulder seen clearly on the horizon and, just before it, take an indistinct path to the left. In a few steps fork left again. Climb steeply to reach the old Coir' a' Ghrunnda path.

Starry Saxifrage

78

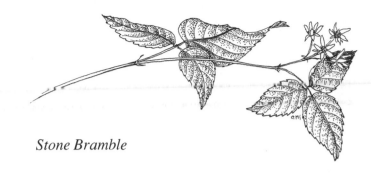

Stone Bramble

3 Proceed along this way, pausing frequently to enjoy the magnificent view seawards; the island of Soay appears to float below, and across the open sea lie the Western Isles. When you first see the entrance to Coir' a' Ghrunnda, follow a path that climbs steeply to the left, hugging the sheer rock face of the skirts of Sron na Ciche.

4 Look up to see the burn descending from the hidden loch above— this is never crossed. Follow the cairned way as it climbs through rough scree and on below large crags. Then the path crosses a massive rock field, keeping well left of large slabs of rock. Look for a narrow gully, which enables you to scramble, with moderate difficulty, up the final band of slabs.

5 Go on along the cairned path as it weaves through more boulders, keeping to the left of the burn. It then comes to the edge of the lovely loch, which is almost entirely surrounded by the towering and castellated sides of Sgurr Alasdair, Sgurr Dubh an Da Bheinn and Sgurr nan Eag. Sit on a boulder overlooking this wonderful corner, deep in the high, remote hills, to observe nature at its most wild and then begin your return—slowly, carefully and faithfully, by the same route.

Practicals

Type of walk: This is a challenging walk. Be prepared to turn back if mist descends or you are intimidated by part of the route.

Distance: 7 miles / 11.2 km
Time: 4–5 hours
Map: OS Landranger 32, South Skye

22

Eas Mor and Coire Lagan

Park in the large space opposite the Glen Brittle Memorial Hut, grid ref. 412217.

Eas Mor is considered to be the grandest waterfall on Skye. It drains Coire na Banachdich and then tumbles for 80 magnificent feet (25m) over the lip of a birch and fern-filled gorge, into a seething pool. The path comes close to the edge of the ravine, with stunning views over the treetops to the fall. Just off the path is a small grassy hollow—the ideal place for a photo-stop or a coffee break.

Loch Coire Lagan

Coire Lagan is considered to be the finest of all the Cuillin corries. In the sheltered basin lies a lovely turquoise-blue lochan. Cross the smooth ice worn boiler-plates of rock, on its shore, to enjoy the reflections in the pool of peaks, pinnacles and soft white cotton-wool clouds—on a good day! To the north east corner of the corrie lies the Great Stone Shoot, where climbers ascend like brightly coloured spiders on their way to Sgurr Alasdair, the highest peak of the Cuillin. Look out over the rim of the corrie to Canna and Rum and, to the Western Isles to see South Uist and Barra.

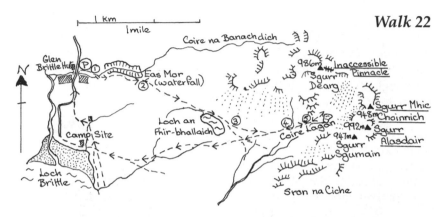

Walk 22

1 Follow the path from the south-east corner of the parking space, heading towards the corner of a small plantation. Cross a small burn, then the Allt Coire na Banachdich on a sturdy wooden bridge, with stiles. Follow the path as it heads off across the moor, with the burn to your left. About 1km from the start the path comes close to the edge of a ravine through which the burn flows, with views across to the waterfall, Eas Mor.

2 Continue to the head of the ravine, where a path, often boggy, branches off to the left into Coire na Banachdich. This walk takes the right branch, which heads along under the steepening slopes of Sgurr Dearg. Soon the path (again quite boggy) runs along the northern shore of the attractive Loch an Fhir-bhallaich.

3 The path then turns southwards and divides—take the left one, though both branches soon join the good path coming up from Glen Brittle campsite. (A lot of restoration work has been done to this path.) Follow the clear way as it begins to climb more steeply, the sight of the rim of Coire Lagan encouraging you to keep going.

Ascend to the left of the Lagan burn which tumbles over the smooth massive slabs of rock. To the right, on the other side of the burn, is the rocky path used by climbers to reach the cliffs of Sron na Ciche.

4 On reaching the brow, you find there is another beyond. Go on over scree and small boulders, coming close to the hurrying stream. At the next brow you realise that there is yet another to surmount, but as the track leads up and over this, there below in a sheltered hollow lies the delightful lochan—a great reward for a longish trek. Here you might spot a pair of ring ouzels.

5 After a pause begin your descent, ignoring your earlier path from the Eas Mor. Pass to the left of Loch an Fhir-bhallaich. Continue on the now improved path. As you come over the brow above the toilet block at the campsite, a landrover track crosses the path. Turn right on this and follow it down through scattered trees to a metal gate by a cottage. Go through, then almost immediately through a metal kissing gate next to a locked gate across the track. There is a sign 'No dogs except on leads' on the gate. The track continues to the road, where you walk straight ahead to the Memorial Hut and your parked car.

Ring Ouzel

Practicals

Type of walk: A challenging walk, with some scrambling.

Distance: 6 miles / 9.7 km
Time: 5 hours
Map: OS Landranger 32

Coire a' Ghreadaidh

Park opposite the youth hostel in Glen Brittle, grid ref. 410225.

Coire a' Ghreadaidh, in the Cuillin, is large and dramatic. Climbers pass through it on their way to scale Sgurr a' Ghreadaidh and Sgurr a' Mhadaidh. It is split into two upper coires (coire meaning 'kettle' in Gaelic), spectacular rough rocky basins of dark gabbro and granite almost completely surrounded by high walls of the parent mountain. These hollows were scoured out by slow-moving glaciers during the last ice age and by ice-plucking at the walls.

Common gulls, seen about the Cuillin, are attracted by the discarded sandwiches of walkers and climbers! The gulls have snow white heads, French grey backs and wings, and their bills are a greenish-yellow and legs yellowish. They have white 'spots' near the tips of their black outer primary feathers.

Coire a' Ghreadaidh

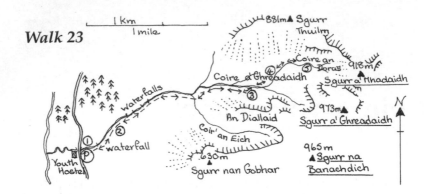

Walk 23

1 km
1 mile

881m▲ Sgurr Thuilm
Coire an Doras 918m
Coire a' Ghreadaidh
Sgurr a' Mhadaidh
waterfalls
An Diallaid
973m▲ Sgurr a' Ghreadaidh
N
Coir' an Eich
waterfall
630m▲ Sgurr nan Gobhar
965m ▲ Sgurr na Banachdich
Youth Hostel

1 Ascend from the parking area, keeping the burn, the Allt a' Choire Ghreadaidh, to your left. It descends in a series of fine waterfalls through a shallow ravine, which is lined with rowan and birch trees. In high summer the moorland on either side supports cross-leaved heath, bog asphodel and heath spotted orchis. The first part of the path has had much work done to it and some of the drains that cross it are wide. These require a large step to cross, others have to be climbed into and then out again.

2 Take care as you follow the path as it winds left along the edge of a ravine and then swings back right, climbing all the time. It follows the burn, with the spur, An Diallaid, ahead and to the right. And then the lower part of the corrie is reached and the view is superb of the jagged rocky peaks of Sgurr a' Ghreadaidh and Sgurr a' Mhadaidh—the former higher and more dramatic; it is the 3rd highest Cuillin.

3 The path comes to the edge of the burn and appears to end. Cross the beck, easily if not in spate, but if it is this is where you will have to start your return. The burn slides over a series of 'boiler' plates, an apt description for the huge smooth whaleback slabs— take care as you cross these because even gabbro rock can be very slippery when wet. Once across continue up the boiler plates beside the burn for a short distance until the path reappears and then winds round and up a moraine, with a fine waterfall below.

4 Go on up the path which continues over grassy areas and occasional bog into Coire an Dorus. This is the more northerly of two inner corries. Thyme, alpine lady's mantle, stone bramble and starry saxifrage thrive over the pebbly ground. The side of Coire an Dorus

curves round and the narrow notch of An Dorus (the Door) between Ghreadaidh and Mhadaidh comes into view at the top of a steep scree slope.

5 This is the end of the outward walk. To continue further requires scrambling and is beyond the remit of this book. Return down the slopes by the route of your ascent, remembering to take care crossing the burn. As you descend enjoy the superb views over Glen Brittle to Rum.

Common Gull

Practicals

Type of walk: This walk visits two corries. It passes pools, waterslides, boiler plates, and dramatic ravines on the ascent culminating in a fine mountain skyline. On your return the views out across to Rum are stupendous.

Distance: 5 miles / 8 km
Time: 4 hours
Map: OS Landranger 32
Harvey's Superwalker Skye: The Cuillin

24

Coire na Creiche and the Fairy Pools

Park in the new forestry car park, grid ref. 424258, below the picnic site marked on the OS map. To reach this, take the minor road to Glen Brittle, leaving the A863 at the turning for Carbost and then turning left again about a mile and a half further on. Look for the parking area on the right after a double bend on the road as it goes down into Glen Brittle.

The Allt Coire a' Mhadaidh has delightful blue-green pools, narrow rapids and water-worn potholes. On its precipitous banks grow holly trees. In autumn these are laden with berries and attract many fieldfares. Further on the waterfalls and pools, known as the Fairy Pools, are set about with rowan, birch and aspen. Here the

Fairy Pool, Coire na Creiche

first waterfall tumbles into an amazing deep turquoise-coloured pool. A second has a delectable pool divided in two by a rock bridge, with the arch underwater. The fairies have good taste—this corner is truly lovely.

The pleasing traverse on the lower slopes of the north-west ridge of Bruach na Frithe is the formerly well used route taken by the climbing pioneers from Sligachan to the Central Cuillin. Below to the left is the wide bowl of Coire na Creiche, the Coire of Spoils, once the site of MacLeod and MacDonald cattle stealing exploits.

Walk 24

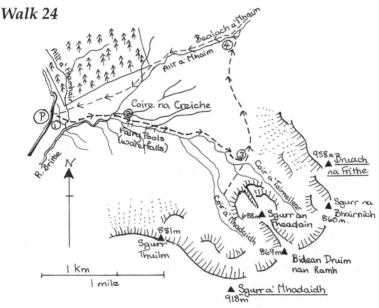

1 Cross the road from the car park and take the path down the grassy bank. Almost immediately fork right on the path which descends towards the burn in Coire na Creiche (the path has been upgraded and is now very good). Cross the Allt an Fhamhair on large slabs of rock. Continue downhill, easily, beside the burn. Directly ahead is the triangular peak of Sgurr an Fheadain, with the dramatic gash of Waterpipe Gully from top to bottom. The coire to the left is Coir' a' Tairneilear, to the right is Coir' a' Mhadaidh. A little further on the new path cuts a corner, where the burn makes a wide bend, and then a tributary burn, the Allt a' Mhaim, has to be crossed on stepping stones. Look here for the green mounds of old dwellings.

87

2 Go up the steep bank on a pitched section of path and then divert from the new path to follow the older way by the river to look at the Fairy Pools. The new path comes to an end here and you should continue on up by the burn. As you approach steeper ground, where the burn exits from Coir' a' Tairneilear, watch out for an easy-to-miss small path off to the left, just before a big scree fan. It climbs up beneath a large boulder to meet a larger path higher up.

3 Walk the delightful dry path, which traverses the lower slopes of the north-west ridge of Bruach na Frithe. Follow the path as it turns a corner and crosses stony ground to reach the lochan at the summit of the Bealach a' Mhaim. Cross the outflow of the lochan to join the path over the bealach at a cairn.

4 Turn left and head downhill for Glen Brittle with its meandering burn. Surprisingly quickly you reach the right-angled corner of pines of the Glen Brittle Forest. The path from now on is excellent. Look left to see Allt Coir' a' Mhadaidh and the Fairy Pools waterfalls from this good vantage point. Cross the Allt an Fhamhair a little higher up than on the outward journey, again on easy flat rocks. Join the outward path and make your way up the path to the road and car park.

Fieldfares

Practicals

Type of walk: This is a lovely walk beside one of the most beautiful rivers on Skye, and with excellent mountain scenery too. The going is good on paths all the way and there is very little climbing.

Distance: 5½ miles / 9 km
Time: 3–4 hours
Map: OS Landranger 32

25

Bruach na Frithe

Take the A863 west from Sligachan for about 5km. Park in a large lay-by, on the left, where the track to Altdearg House leaves the road, left, grid ref. 479297. It is made obvious by the wheelie bins for the house rather than by the small discreet sign 'Footpath to Glen Brittle'.

Bruach na Frithe (brae of the forest) is reputedly the easiest of the Cuillins to climb, and it is suggested that it can be done with hands in pockets. It is nevertheless a very fine climb and a beautiful hill; and because of its position at the bend in the Cuillin Ridge it commands possibly the best views in both directions. All the usual cautions about climbing Munros apply. It should not be taken lightly just because it is not so difficult as some others! In particular it is very easy to get lost in mist and then you could find yourself in some very uncomfortable places.

It is not a good plan in the Cuillin to wait for the mist to clear—it may take several days. Also the compass is unreliable because

Bruach na Frithe in snow

of the magnetic rock. It is mainly gabbro which is enjoyably rough and adhesive, but on these northern Cuillin, in particular, there is much dolerite and basalt (usually in the form of geological dykes) which gets very slippery in wet conditions. So choose a good day and turn back if you are worried.

Walk 25

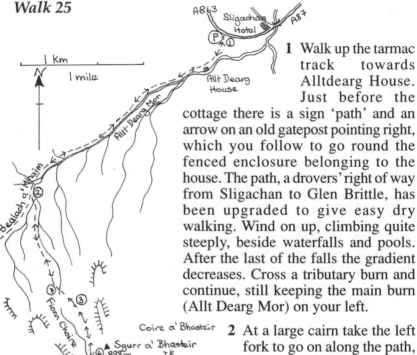

1 Walk up the tarmac track towards Alltdearg House. Just before the cottage there is a sign 'path' and an arrow on an old gatepost pointing right, which you follow to go round the fenced enclosure belonging to the house. The path, a drovers' right of way from Sligachan to Glen Brittle, has been upgraded to give easy dry walking. Wind on up, climbing quite steeply, beside waterfalls and pools. After the last of the falls the gradient decreases. Cross a tributary burn and continue, still keeping the main burn (Allt Dearg Mor) on your left.

2 At a large cairn take the left fork to go on along the path, which is marked by small cairns. Cross a subsidiary burn easily on rocks. Soon the path begins to climb more steeply up to the lip of the Fionn Choire, with its burn, Allt an Fhionn Choire, descending in a fine waterfall in a ravine to your left. Just before the lip of the corrie follow the path across the burn at a point where it makes a wide bend to the right. Climb the bank on the far side where there is a cairn. Continue on into the lower corrie where the path becomes less distinct on grass and moraine. Head for a small ravine towards the left side of the back of the corrie to pick up the path again on the left.

3 Ascend the zig-zagging path into the boulder-strewn upper corrie,

90

which is almost devoid of vegetation. Follow the burn on up towards the shoulder on the left (east) side. (The burn rises at 825m and is the highest flowing water in the Cuillin—worth knowing on a hot day!) Pick you way up the boulder-strewn slopes until you reach the Bealach na Lice. From here you have an amazing view of Am Basteir and the Basteir Tooth.

4 Turn right (west) and head for Bruach na Frithe by the small path which contours under a small rocky peak—Sgurr a' Fionn Choire. Follow this and gain the ridge beyond it. Watch out here for ptarmigan (and also in Fionn Choire). Walk on up the relatively broad and fairly gentle ridge to the summit, skirting a rocky tower on the left (Lota Corrie) side. The summit is marked by a cylindrical concrete trig point—the only one on the Cuillin Ridge. Pause here to enjoy the magnificent viewpoint.

5 To return, retrace your steps towards Sgurr a' Fionn Choire. Bypass this on the left and traverse the rocky slopes to the ridge which leads out onto Sgurr a' Bhasteir. Peer down into Coire a' Bhasteir to see the tiny lochan and the Basteir Gorge from above.

6 Leave the ridge before it starts to climb again and descend into Fionn Choire. Pick your way down to find the path beside the burn. Descend the rough boulder-strewn upper corrie, follow the path above the burn as it goes through a small ravine. The burn then flows away to the left and disappears. Continue across the rather featureless grassy morrain, heading for the distant spur beyond the corrie lip where you crossed the burn. Cairns mark the path again as it approaches the burn crossing.

7 Follow the clear path all the way back to the Sligachan path, where you turn right to retrace your steps to Allt Dearg House and the parking area.

Practicals

Type of walk: See first two paragraphs.

Distance:	8 miles / 13 km
Time:	6–7 hours
Map:	OS Landranger 32
	Harvey's Superwalker 'Skye: The Cuillin'

26

Coire a' Bhasteir Gorge

Park 250yds/230m south-west of the Sligachan Hotel, grid ref. 485298.

The scenery on the road north as you approach Sligachan is of the magnificent Cuillin, a vast ridge of jagged peaks and hidden corries. The few houses that lie close-by seem toy-like against the massive flanks of the hills. **Coire a' Bhasteir Gorge** is an exciting, rocky wilderness, forming an impressive foreground to the pinnacles of Sgurr nan Gillean.

Bhasteir Gorge and pinnacle ridge of Sgurr nan Gillean

In summer, as you enter this mountain fastness, its harshness is softened by large clumps of **alpine lady's mantle**, covered with pale-lemon flowers. This small perennial thrives in mountainous parts, mainly from Yorkshire northwards. The leaves are cut to the base into five or seven oblong leaflets, which are clothed, on the underside, with white silky hairs which gives the leaves a silvery appearance.

1 Cross the road and take the reinforced path opposite for 230yds/ 200m over the peat and heather moorland to the narrow bridge over the Allt Dearg Mor. Once over the cascading burn, follow the cairned path that meanders on to come to the side of the Allt Dearg Beag— your lively pleasing companion for the remainder of the walk.

2 Walk upstream to pass several dramatic waterfalls, where the stream descends between heather and fern, shaded by aspens, birch and rowan. The Allt Dearg Beag comes down in great haste, a deep turquoise river that foams and sparkles as it races over its rocky bed. In spate it rages and boils but it can be a gentle burn, and then you can sit on the huge rocks and enjoy your sandwiches. The pinnacles of Sgurr nan Gillean seem to tower directly

Walk 26

Sligachan
A863 Hotel
A87
Allt Dearg House
R. Sligachan
1 Km
1 mile
Allt Dearg Beag
Sgurr a' Bhasteir 898m
Coire a' Bhasteir
Am Basteir 934m.
Sgurr nan Gillean 964m.

Alpine Lady's Mantle

93

above the streaming water. Ignore the bridge over the burn. Pause here to look across the moorland towards Portree, the Storr and across to Dun Caan on Raasay. Ascend steadily towards the spectacular gorge.

3 Follow faithfully the cairned way, climbing steadily beside the burn. The path leads you into the spectacular ravine and is easy at first but soon progress will become too difficult for most walkers and this will be the point of your return.

4 Return by the same route.

Ptarmigan in spring plumage

Practicals

Type of walk: A steady climb to one of Skye's wildest gorges, with fine views and a dancing burn to help you on your way.

Distance: 5 miles / 8 km
Time: 3½ hours
Map: OS outdoor Leisure 32

27

Sgurr nan Gillean (south-east ridge)

Park as for walk 26—200 metres south-west of the Sligachan Hotel, grid ref. 485298.

The name, **Sgurr nan Gillean** means 'peak of the young men' but whatever age or sex you are attempt as much of the exhilarating ascent as you feel happy with. The way up is often described as the tourist route—for the first part it could be described as such but beyond Coire Riabhach the ascent is harder and should not be undertaken lightly or attempted in the mist. Its conical tip, seen from the parking area and beyond, is most people's ideal shape of a mountain. It is a magnificent mountain and from its summit the views are peerless.

1 From the parking area, cross the road to take an upgraded path over the moorland for 200yds/180m, to a narrow bridge over the Allt Dearg Mor. Beyond the bridge, the path soon leaves the burn and continues over heather moorland, rising gently on a much improved route. This brings you to the side of the Allt Dearg Beag from where you have a good view of its lovely waterfalls. Walk upstream and then cross the burn on a narrow footbridge.

2 Go on along a continuing path (south), across a cairned shoulder above Nead na h-Iolaire and to the rim of Coire Riabhach. Pause by the cairn to enjoy a retrospect view of the Old Man of Storr and of Dun Caan on Raasay. Ahead lies a necklace of lochans, Loch a' Choire Riabhaich, Lochan Dubha and Loch an Athain. Look sideways to spot the peaks of Glamaig, Marsco and Bla Bheinn.

3 This may be the point for some walkers to start their two-mile return. The more adventurous will wish to go on to follow the narrow, indistinct but cairned path that descends slightly, into the corrie. It passes west of the lochan in the bowl, over some rocky humps and then climbs a clear path through a scree-filled gully. At the top of

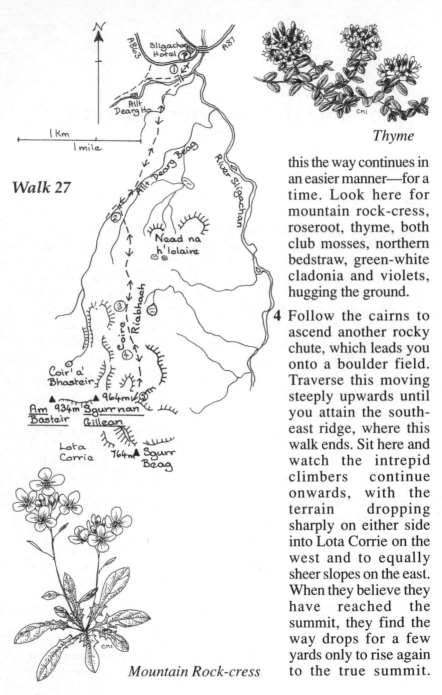

Walk 27

Thyme

Mountain Rock-cress

this the way continues in an easier manner—for a time. Look here for mountain rock-cress, roseroot, thyme, both club mosses, northern bedstraw, green-white cladonia and violets, hugging the ground.

4 Follow the cairns to ascend another rocky chute, which leads you onto a boulder field. Traverse this moving steeply upwards until you attain the southeast ridge, where this walk ends. Sit here and watch the intrepid climbers continue onwards, with the terrain dropping sharply on either side into Lota Corrie on the west and to equally sheer slopes on the east. When they believe they have reached the summit, they find the way drops for a few yards only to rise again to the true summit.

From your viewing platform, with your back tucked safely against a rock, watch the climbers on the nearby pinnacles and listen to their conversations across the abysses between. They disturb the mountain silence so much that the ravens, inhabitants of the tops, fly around croaking angrily.

5 Return by your outward route.

Heather

Practicals

Type of walk: There are several ways to attain the south-west ridge, the one above is the easiest route, but not one to be underestimated.

Distance:	8 miles / 12.8 km
Time:	6–7 hours
Map:	OS Landranger 32
	Harvey's Superwalker, Skye, The Cuillin

28

Sligachan to Coruisk

Park in the large lay-by close to the Sligachan Hotel, grid ref. 487299.

The 7½ miles to **Loch Coruisk** have been described as the longest in Scotland. It is the most famous walk on the island and requires immense determination to complete it. Look for ravens, sandpipers, meadow pipits and wheatears as you go and, once at Coruisk watch for common gulls and terns. Here, on a long summer's day, when the sun is shining, this magical hollow in the hills becomes a secluded sun-trap and is an especial corner of Skye, perhaps the loveliest.

Captain Maryon's Cairn, reached by half a mile's walking, left, from Druim Hain, stands about 10ft high on a square base. It was erected by a friend of the captain. Large boulders of gabbro form the base of the pyramid and the stones that taper up to its top become progressively smaller. Apparently Maryon set out on a walk from Sligachan and never returned. His skeleton was found at this lonely spot 18 months later.

Loch Coruisk

Walk 28

1 Walk to the old road bridge and follow the signposted path in the direction of Loch Coruisk. The path, with the pretty Allt Dairich to your left for a short distance, has been well reinforced. Continue on the good way through Glen Sligachan, with convenient boulders to cross small burns that tumble down the hillside to join, below you to the right, the River Sligachan. To the right, the glen is dominated by the shapely Sgurr nan Gillean.

2 After nearly 2 miles/ 3km the Allt na Measarroch is reached. Walk down towards the river until you find a suitable place to cross. Continue on below the slopes of Marsco, which almost hides the dark forbidding bulk of Bla Bheinn.

3 After 4 miles/6km from Sligachan, the path divides just before Ruadh Stac, which lies to your left and beyond Marsco. The left fork leads down to Camusunary, the right to Loch Coruisk and this is the path you need. Head across the glen and then ascend the well-worn path that begins its steep ascent to the summit of the ridge, called

99

Druim Hain. The rock strewn path is generally dry and a great relief after the earlier route. Sit by the cairn at the top of your climb and enjoy the dramatic views of the Cuillin.

4 A path going off left leads towards Sgurr Hain and you may wish to take this for ½ a mile to see, below on the right, Captain Maryon's monument. Return to the cairn at Druim Hain to begin the long descent to Loch Coruisk. On the way pause to look down on Loch a' Choire Riabhaich, with its waterfall below.

5 Continue on down the rather indistinct way, savouring the views of the open sea to Soay and Rum. Nearer the shore of Coruisk the path leads to stepping stones. One row leads to a small island and another to the other side. Sometimes the stones are under water and you should not attempt to cross (people have drowned here) but hopefully you will be able to and to sit on the great whalebacks of rock and just enjoy Loch Coruisk and its little islands. Look up at the great mass of the Cuillin slashed with white as many rivulets race down sheer slopes.

6 All that now remains is to go back to the Sligachan Hotel by the same route—7½ long and hard miles, taking up to 4 hours to complete; that is for the return walk only!

Common Sandpiper

Practicals

Type of walk: This is a challenging 15 mile hard walk requiring good boots, waterproofs and sufficient food and drink. It is an expedition for the strong fell walker.

Distance: 15 miles / 25 km
Time: 8 hours
Map: OS Landranger 32

29

Marsco from Loch Ainort

Park on the right (east) side of the A87, the Broadford to Sligachan road, in a large lay-by just north of the bridge over the Allt Coire nam Bruadaran, grid ref. 534267.

The mountains of the **Black Cuillin**, with their jagged, peaks, are composed mainly of gabbro. This is a rock that gives an excellent adhesive grip on the soles of your walking boots but, when scrambling, can be tough on your hands, knees, seat and clothes. Its steeper slopes do not support grass or heather. The fine smooth shapes of the **Red Hills** contrast starkly with the Black Cuillin. These are hills of granite which is more acid than gabbro. During weathering much scree forms on both. The Red Hills lie to the east of Sligachan Glen and the Black Cuillin to the west.

Marsco, one of the Red Hills, is the striking conical-shaped hill seen from Glen Sligachan. It is a rare Red Hill in that it is blessed with little scree.

Marsco from Sligachan

1 Cross the road and take one of the many paths, on the right of the burn. Climb to the top of the spectacular waterfall, above which the water slides over enormous granite 'boiler plates'. Here the paths become more united. Go on walking upstream, with the burn

on your left. *Walk 29*

The often very wet path, little more than a sheep trod, continues up the glen. In August the mire on either side is colourful with bog asphodel and heath spotted orchis. As the trod gets higher keep as close as possible to

the bank of the burn to avoid the worst of the wet. Cross several tributary burns as you go.

2 After about a mile up the glen the Allt Mam a' Phobuill joins the Allt Coire nam Bruadaran from the right. Cross this easily on stones and continue up beside the now much smaller Bruadaran, towards a long waterfall seen in the distance below a low col. To the right of the col is Marsco and the objective of this walk.

3 Climb up onto the gentle spur, to the right of the waterfall, and follow an indistinct path which takes you up onto the bealach— the path becomes rockier as you ascend and the stream smaller. At the top of the bealach there is a line of old metal fence posts which you follow.

4 Turn right with the fence posts and strike up the south-east ridge of Marsco. The ridge is rocky with outcrops of shattered granite which is rough and good to walk. Various paths zig-zag up the steep way—choose your preferred line. Above the granite outcrops the rock suddenly changes and the slope becomes quite grassy. Then the ridge narrows and where the fence posts go straight up an outcrop go left on a very clear path, which diminishes gradually. Scramble up a rather steep grass and rock bank to reach the top of the level grassy ridge. Descend to a little grassy col where the

102

fence posts (old friends by now) suddenly turn right and go down over the edge. (Remember this place for your return route.)

5 Go ahead up a broad grassy slope. Then the way suddenly narrows dramatically to a very sharp almost level ridge, which takes you to the summit cairn. Walk this way with care—and not at all if there is a gale blowing. From here the views are superb and you can see both the Red and Black Cuillin.

Bog Asphodel

C.H.Isherwood

6 To return, retrace your steps to the grassy dip noted earlier. Head down to the left from the lowest point of the dip, just before you reach the fence posts. Zig-zag down the very steep grass, avoiding eroded areas. Then when the slope eases traverse to the left below scree, still keeping company with the fence posts, across towards Coire nan Laogh, where you walk along its outer lip. Head towards the burn, the Allt Coire nan Laogh, aiming for a crossing point before it enters a ravine. Traverse round the far bank on animal tracks to ground which is less steep and then descend easily to the col— Mam a' Phobuill. This is the col Bonny Prince Charlie is said to have used when escaping across Skye.

7 At the col the indistinct path you have been following joins a good track—but this track turns left for Sligachan. This walk turns right on drier ground at the far side of the col, picking up traces of path and animal tracks again, and heading for two large boulders on the skyline. Continue round the hillside, past the boulders, descending gently but keeping well above the ravines of descending burns, until below the nose of Ciche na Beinne Deirge. Here go steeply down a grassy spur to reach the bank of the Allt Mam a' Phobuill after it has emerged from its ravine. Go on down with the burn to your right, into the glen, to its confluence with the Allt Coire nam Bruadaran.

8 Turn left and follow your outward route back to the waterfall and the parking area.

Heath Spotted Orchid

Practicals

Type of walk: This is one for a good day and preferably after a dry spell. There is no difficulty at any stage but it is a hard slog both up and down.

Distance: 6 miles / 9.6 km
Time: 5–6 hours
Map: OS Landranger 32

Kilmarie to Elgol and Camasunary, round walk

Park in a large parking area on the Elgol road (B8083), just beyond Kirkibost, grid ref. 545172, opposite the path to Camasunary.

If time allows walk across the close-cropped, springy turf of the lovely, curving Camasunary Bay. Pause here to enjoy the gannets diving out at sea and **Manx shearwaters** skimming above the top of the waves. These birds are probably from Rum where there is the largest colony in the western world. Shags, too, fly close to the water. Look for families of eiders snoozing on the quiet waters of the bay. Among the rocks sandpipers call to their brood and then fly ahead to scold from the top of rocks. At the far end of the beach is an open bothy where you are invited to enter—very useful for shelter during a sudden squall.

The return from **Camasunary to Kirkibost** is a vehicular track, reinforced by the army in the 1960s. In spite of its directness and general roughness there are dramatic views to be enjoyed of Bla Bheinn. Stop on the brow and look back to see more of the Cuillin and your last view of the magical bay. In summer the moorland is decked with the woolly seed heads of cotton grass. Spearwort, lousewort and milkwort grow delightfully among the pungent smelling bog myrtle.

Cullin and Loch Scavaig from Elgol

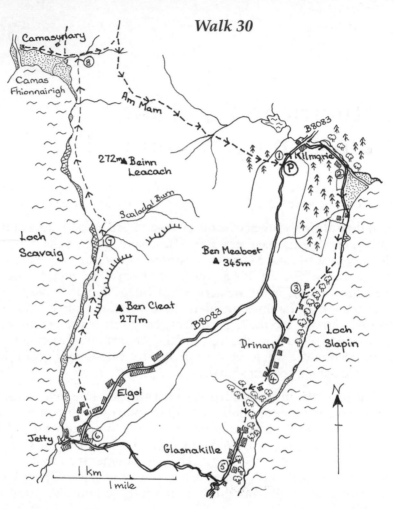

1 Walk back, north-east, for a short distance towards Kirkibost. Opposite a cottage and just before the stone bridge over the Abhainn Cille Mhaire, turn right down a road signed 'Old Kilmarie and Graveyard'. Cross a cattle grid and carry on down beside the burn, which is flanked with alders. Go on past an old kennels on the left. The road continues past, on the right, a large white house with a walled garden. To the left the burn hurries on beneath mature trees; it is all very ordered and quite lovely.

2 Follow the road, right, along the shore and at its end there is a small white house, just beyond a slipway on the shore. Take a track that leads off uphill just to the right of this dwelling. Go on up the track and keep straight on, ignoring another which soon branches off on the right to another cottage. Follow the track as it goes up and round the headland, giving lovely views over Loch Slapin. Pass through a tall kissing gate and then past a ruined stone building. Continue uphill.

3 There is a white house above on your right, the first of the next settlement (Drinan). The way comes up to meet the reinforced track leading to this house, and you turn away from this—left along the continuing way. Carry on through a metal gate, ignore a track leading off on the left and go through another gate. Soon you reach another stretch of metalled road, where it makes a large bend. Go straight ahead, above the settlement of Drinan, with more fine views out to sea.

4 The metalled road ends at a little turning area above a white croft house on the left. Continue ahead on a fine grassy track (with Torrin marble in the ruts) to pass through a metal gate. Beyond a new bungalow, the track becomes a grassy path going down below birch and hazel, through another gate to a bridge over the burn, Allt na Cille. Continue along the fern-lined way and through tall ash, and then stride the path as it goes uphill between coppiced hazel. Once through another gate you join a broader track, with a house to the left and, beyond its driveway, you meet a metalled road again, at a turning place.

5 Stroll the road as it runs along above the coast with the houses of Glasnakille on both sides. At the telephone box, turn right and follow the road over the moor, past a signal station. As you reach the brow Gars-bheinn appears, and there are superb views over to Rum, Eigg and Canna. Then it's downhill towards Elgol.

6 At the B8083, turn right and climb uphill for 330 yards/300m to a signposted track, leading off left. Go by some houses, and then proceed along a fenced path to reach open terrain. Walk on and begin a descent towards the cliff edge. Then the way traverses the steep slopes of Ben Cleat, with wonderful views across Loch Scavaig, the path coming close to the cliff edge, where you should walk with care.

7 Follow the path as it continues beneath the crags of Carn Mor. Gradually the way begins to descend into Glen Scaladal, a quiet

valley with a wide beach. Ford the
Scaladal Burn as it crosses the
greensward above the beach.
Ascend left from the beach on a
narrow path. This comes very close
to the cliff edge and great care
should be taken as you proceed
below Beinn Leacach.
Eventually the path begins to
descend towards turf-edged
Camasunary Bay. Cross the
tumbling Abhainn nan Leac
by boulders or, if in spate,
walk upstream to a bridge.

Manx
Shearwaters

8 If you decide to view, rather than explore Camasunary, turn right
beyond the footbridge to begin your ascent of a track. Follow this
rough way, without looking back, to the high point near Am Mam
and then turn round to enjoy the superb view of the Camasunary
Bay. Continue on following the track, with your route in no doubt
to eventually arrive at the parking area on the opposite side of the
B-road.

Practicals

*Type of walk: This is a long ramble and should be attempted
when you have a full day for walking. It is a walk of great
contrasts. The east side of the peninsula is more settled and
crofted, more sheltered and with more trees, although there are
bleak moorland areas. The views are pleasant but not nearly
so spectacular as the cliff path to Camasunary, one of Skye's
most dramatic stretches, where in parts you should walk with
extreme caution . The return over the track to the parking area,
is rough underfoot, but you are in no doubt of your route.*

Distance:	11 miles / 17.7 km
Time:	6–7 hours
Map:	OS Landranger 32
NB:	The walk could be done in 'there and back' sections if you don't want to do the whole round.

Boreraig and Suisnish

Park at Camas Malag on grass by the shore, grid ref. 583193. This is reached by following the B8083 from Broadford, along Strath Suardal. Half a mile beyond Loch Cill Chriosd, turn off the B-road where it veers right and continue on the narrower road until the end of the tarmac.

Torrin Marble was formed when the limestone along the boundary with the Beinn an Dubhaich granite was metamorphosed (came under great heat). The white marble was in great demand as a decorative stone and a railway line transported it from the quarries at Suardal to Broadford for shipping elsewhere. The trucks were horse-drawn and in 1911 the company bought a small steam engine to pull the wagons. Alas by 1912 the quarry was closed and the railway removed.

Limestone is a tough whitish rock which is partly soluble in rainwater. Exposed surfaces become gradually eroded. Water

Loch Slapin and Bla Bheinn from Camas Malag

trickles between gaps, or joints, in the rock and these may become deep grooves, or grykes. These are separated by furrowed blocks with ridges, or clints. Small plants, such as dog's mercury, herb robert, wood sage and various ferns, thrive in the shelter provided by the clints.

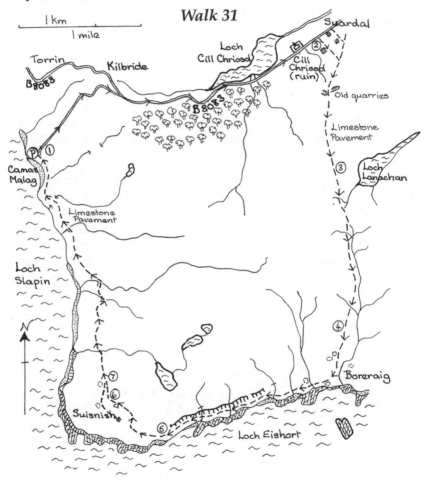

Walk 31

1 Walk back up the tarmacked road, with the present Torrin Marble Quarry away to your left, until you reach the main road (B8083). Turn right and walk in the direction of Broadford. Mixed deciduous trees cover the low hills to your right. After a mile you pass, on your left, the shallow Loch Cill Chriosd. In summer white water

110

Mountain Avens

lilies flower amid the reeds and the lovely waters are frequented by mallard, heron and dabchick. At other times of the year the loch is visited by whooper swans. Just beyond the loch, on a knoll on the left, stands the ruined church, Cill Chriosd. Opposite in a large lay-by are boards detailing the formation and extraction of Torrin Marble.

2 Continue on to take, on the right, a track that climbs steadily. Go past buildings and then cross a field to join another track which follows the line of the old mineral railway. Turn right to walk on through the old workings where the marble was extracted. Go on through an area of limestone pavement. In summer spring cinquefoil, mountain avens, carpets of thyme and fairy flax delight the eye. Go on uphill on a pleasing green track.

Stonechats

3 Once over the top of the hill the rock changes and the vegetation becomes acid, heather moor and bog. Climb a new stile into an area which at the time of writing has just been planted with native trees. A board asks you to keep to the indistinct wet path. Loch Lanachan lies to the left. Continue on the path which runs along the side of a valley where you might spot stonechats and golden plover. Ahead lies Loch Eishort.

4 The path descends gently to the ruined settlement of Boreraig, 'cleared' in the nineteenth century. Sit on the grassy rocks by the shore for your picnic and watch for sandpipers, oystercatchers and seals. Then walk west above the shoreline, heading for the base of distant cliffs. Cross a stone slab bridge over a burn and follow the path over another burn. Descend gently to stroll the short turf of a wide wave-cut platform below the cliffs. The path wanders, easily, up and down, along this for about two miles. Look for the waterfalls that cascade down the cliffs and enjoy the splendid view out over the sea to Rum.

5 Finally the path rounds a large outcrop and begins to ascend steadily to the top of the cliff. Here the views are even wider and you can see Bla Bheinn. At a Y-junction, take the right branch. This leads to a field with a barn and sheep pens. Look for the sign by the fence directing you right for Kilbride. Follow the field boundary round, uphill at first. Turn left with it and descend a short way into a valley, where you cross a burn. Take the obvious path, through the bracken, up the far side. Look over the field boundary to see the old deserted settlement of Suisnish, another casualty of the 'clearances'.

6 At the top of the hill there is a gate in the fence but do not pass through. Turn right instead and walk above the fence, enjoying the views as you go, across Loch Slapin to Bla Bheinn. After a short distance the path descends to join the track from Suisnish.

7 Walk the track, with Loch Slapin below to your left. The track curves inland and crosses two burns. Go on over more limestone pavement and follow the way as it descends to the glorious bay of Camas Malag.

Practicals

Type of walk: This is a long circuit, which is full of interest. It crosses limestone pavement and acidic bog. It passes through moorland hills, along the seashore and traverses cliffs from where you can expect to enjoy spectacular views. Choose a good day.

Distance:	11 miles / 17 km
Time:	5–6 hours
Map:	OS Outdoor Leisure 8

Point of Sleat

Park at the end of the road, near the old church of Aird, grid ref. 589007. There is limited space and, as this is a turning area, please park considerately.

Sleat, pronounced slate, is the 'foot' of Skye. It stretches out to sea in a south-westerly direction towards the islands of Rum and Eigg. It is often called 'the Garden of Skye' because, along its easterly shore, there are woodlands, lush gardens and good farmland. The walk to the Point of Sleat leaves this lushness behind as it traverses the Aird, but in the sheltered ravines flourish luxuriant ferns, low growing shrubs and colourful flowers. The view from Acairseid an Rubha is a delight but that from the Point, the southernmost tip of Skye, surpasses it. Here you can look across to Eigg, Rum, Coll and Tiree; to Moidart, Morar and Ardnamurchan; and to the Cuillin.

Lighthouse, Point of Sleat

1 Go through the gate at the end of the road to walk the good track that swings out over the moorland, passing through great banks of ling and heath. Look for golden-ringed dragonflies darting over the boggy pools between the plants. Follow the way to the top of the brow to see, to the west, the islands of Rum and Eigg. Descend

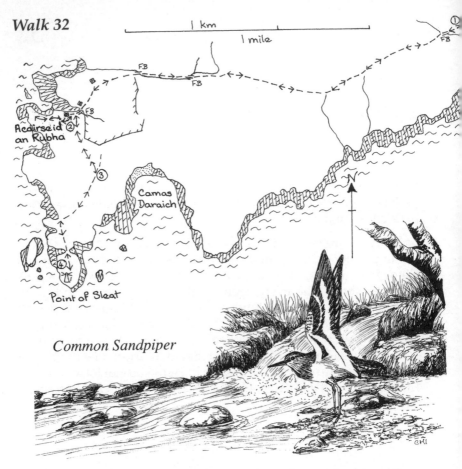

Common Sandpiper

to a wooden bridge and go on and on along the continuing path as it gently rises and falls to reach a gate. Stride on beside a burn, crossed twice by footbridges, which hurries through a steep-sided ravine. Pass a house to come to a hidden bay and a tiny harbour. Go through a gate to a dwelling on the quayside and opposite, begin your scramble up a faint path onto the fine headland of Arcaiseid an Rubha. Pause by the cairns to enjoy the incredible view.

2 Return to the path and to the cottage on the quay. Do not walk down to the little harbour but turn right before the bridge over a burn. Climb a rocky staircase, keeping in line with a wire fence to the left. Where you spot a small bay to the right and the fence turns

left, swing away south east and follow a wettish way up a low heather slope above the valley bottom. Make your way along the shoulder to a col overlooking Camas Daraich. Look for red-throated divers here swimming and diving for fish in the clear blue water.

3 Then a good path appears. Follow this to the top of some concrete steps and, encouraged by the first view of the lighthouse, descend to a small bay. Go on along a stone causeway through a rocky ravine to cross a narrow spit, with sea on either side. This links the Point with the mainland. Climb the steps ahead. These lead to a path through bracken to a grassy sward beyond which is the white-washed, unmanned sturdy lighthouse.

4 Return by the same route.

Red-throated Divers

Practicals

Type of walk: There is a pleasing track and path to the headland, Acairseid an Rubha, from where there are fine views. Some walkers may be happy to go no further but the views from the Point are even more stunning. From the headland to the Point the path, as seen on the OS map, is indistinct and often wet in places. Aim for higher ground in the direction of the Point and choose the driest way.

Distance: 6 miles / 10 km
Time: 4 hours
Maps: OS Landranger 32

33

Dalavil wood and deserted village

Drive south on the A851, down the Sleat peninsula. Take the road signed Achnacloich and Tarskavaig just after Kilbeg. After 1½miles/ 3km there is a clear track with a metal barrier across it, on the left. A little further on up the hill is a large passing place with room to park and a notice 'Clan Donald Lands. Sheep live on this hill. Please control your dog if walking'. Grid ref. 623068.

It was not the Clearances that emptied **Dalavil** but the Education Acts of the 1870s. Attendance at school was made obligatory and it was cheaper to remove the crofters rather than build a school in the settlement. The children would have had a ten mile walk each day to reach the nearest township and there was no road out of Dalavil, only a path.

Coille Dalavil, the lovely ancient wood by Loch a'Ghlinne is owned and managed by the Clan Donald Lands Trust and was deer-fenced in 1994 to allow the trees to regenerate. It is along the clear track

Rowan Rock, Dalavil

(with the barrier across), which runs to the first area deer fenced, that this walk starts.

Loch a' Ghlinne is an extensive stretch of water, much of it colonised with white water lilies and great reed. Here fish leap. Herons stand motionless in the shallow water. In winter it hosts whooper swans. This too has been fenced, the high wire mesh enclosing the loch and the woodland.

Whooper swans

Walk 33

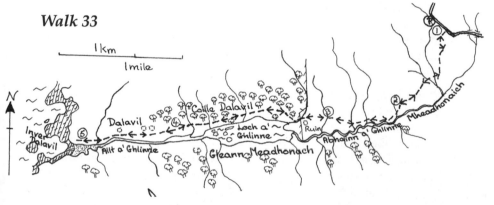

1 Walk back from the lay-by to take the track, now on your right. Go round the barrier and descend down and down. Wade the ford and continue on the reinforced track. After crossing a narrow burn you arrive at a fenced area of young trees. At its far corner the track ceases.

2 Look ahead from here to see the wheel marks of a vehicle, steadily descending, diagonally, towards the river and your first magical sighting of Loch a' Ghlinne with the sea beyond. On a sunny day they both sparkle and are silvery. Follow the tracks until they cross the river. Here the walker ignores the deep ford and continues along the nearside bank of the Dalavil. Cross a small burn at the easiest point and continue parallel with the river until you reach another ford, where tyre tracks reveal that the vehicle has re-crossed.

3 Follow the tracks across a rather wet pasture and head for a ruined croft, its chimney almost intact. It stands by a solitary ash, with several sheep pens close by. Beyond, pass through the deer gate and follow the vehicle tracks across a small stream and then pasture into Dalavil wood, to follow an ancient path. Pass beneath scots pine, birch, ash and oak and on under numerous beech. Here look for rowan and scots pine seedlings, and for tiny beech seedlings sprouting from moss covered fallen trunks.

4 Eventually the track emerges from the trees and a narrow path continues to a gate through the deer fence. To the left, across a wide grassy tract of land, lies the 'canal' built to drain the land and channel the water from the loch out to sea. The path carries on beside a ruined wall and keeps just above the wide damp hinterland of the canal. It leads to another ruin and then the remains of others that formed the settlement of Dalavil. From here walk along the track for a few yards and then take an indistinct path to the right that skirts the higher ground to the north. This is the path that leads to the beach. Keep along it until you reach a heather-clad outcrop, one of many above the shore.

5 Stand here and enjoy the second magical moment of the walk— when Inver Dalavil lies at your feet. Here gentle waves lap the many small islands across the bay. Oyster catchers, curlews and greater black-backed gulls abound. To the right you can see the Red and Black Cuillin, Soay, Rum and Eigg. It is a wonderful reward for the walker who has made the 4 mile trek—but don't forget that it is four miles back again.

Practicals

Type of walk: This is a pleasing walk but, in parts, it can be wet underfoot. There is no obvious path but sheep trods and the lure of the distant loch, and the sea, keep you in the right direction. The ancient woodland of Dalavil is a delight.

Distance: 8 miles / 12.8 km
Time: 4 hours
Map: OS Landranger 32

34

Three short walks in Sleat—
Fairy Glen, Dunscaith Castle, Ord

Fairy Glen

Drive on the A851 towards Armadale pier. Continue through the village of Ardvasar and, after the de-restriction sign, take the next right turn. A few yards along park in a large lay-by, on the right, grid ref. 627027.

1 Return to the A-road and turn right. Walk on a few yards to a gap in the hedge, on the left and before a bridge. Descend three steps and then go through a gate which gives access to the Fairy Glen. Walk the narrow path that descends steadily below hazel, oak and alder. To your right a small burn tumbles foam-topped, descending in a pleasing cascade.

Walk 34 I

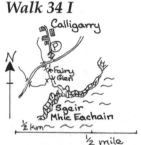

Common Terns

2 Follow the narrow path as it runs high above the burn to pass, on the opposite bank, a stream plummeting in three fine falls. Continue on down the easy way. Where the trees open out you can glimpse the Sound of Sleat. The path follows the curve of the burn and here another delightful fall carries the racing water over the drop in its bed. Where the path enters the bay, hazel, willow, alder, ash and aspen cover the cliffs above.

3 Once on the shore explore this secret corner at the foot of this delectable narrow glen. Out to sea, you might spot terns diving to skim the water for fish, shrieking harshly. Look for the cleft at the foot of the cliffs that almost encircle the beach. In the constant spray that falls from above grow luxuriant ferns, willow, aspen, alder and ragged robin.

Return by the same route.

Practicals	
Distance:	1 mile / 1.6 km
Time:	1 hour
Map:	OS Landranger 32

Dunscaith Castle

Drive along the A851 in the direction of Armadale Pier and, after Isleornsay, take the right turn for Ord and Tokavaig. Pass through both settlements and continue to Ob (Bay) Gauscavaig. Park in one of the largish lay-bys on the side of the bay opposite the castle, grid ref. 595115.

The ruined **Dunscaith Castle** stands on a rocky headland, on the northern tip of the bay, a good position from which to defend the entrance to Loch Eishort. It is surrounded by sea on three sides. Until late in the sixteenth century Dunscaith was the home of the MacDonalds. All that is left today are two arches that once supported a bridge. The latter spanned a ravine that connected the mainland with the isolated rock. Beyond the arches a row of stone steps leads up to a grassy summit within remnants of walls.

Dunscaith Castle

1 Walk back (north) along the narrow road, with the castle to your left, to take, on the left, a gated track. Where it ends, just before a cottage, bear left and follow one of the grassy tracks to the foot of the fortification.

2 Do not attempt to cross the 'bridge'—the ruins, though listed, are not maintained. A safer approach can be made by an easy scramble from the beach to the side of the 'bridge'.

Walk 34 II

Ord

Park on the shore at Ord, grid ref. 615133. (Follow instructions above for Dunscaith Castle)

Jonathan MacDonald in his book *Discovering Skye* says "**Ord** is one of the most scenic, peaceful and delectably beautiful townships in Skye with its awe-inspiring views of mountain and sea". All walkers will agree with him.

Walk 34 III

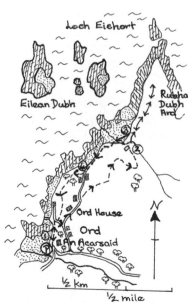

1 From the parking area, walk north (sea to the left) along a short grassy track to a junction with a narrow road. Turn sharp right and climb uphill. Turn left to pass Ord House and wind on to take, on the right, a track leading off over the grassy slopes. Carry on along this pleasing way. Continue where the track begins to bear right and descends steadily to a glen. Follow the way, now a grassy track, as it veers left and runs along the valley towards a white house on the shore.

2 Keep well right of the dwelling, step across a stream that runs in front of the house. Bear right here to scramble up the shallow cliffs to sit on a boulder and enjoy the view. Across Loch Eishort you can see where you

Common Seal

walked from Boreraig to Suisnish (walk 31). In the waters below you, look for an island with brilliant green grass carpeting a huge boulder. Beneath it, is a coral beach that seems to have its own built-in sunshine. On the next island you might spot dozens of basking seals.

3 Return down the slope to the beach and cross in front of the house. Step across the stream and walk on along a fine green sward to the foot of a little headland. Follow a path as it climbs a short bouldery way on to the top of the low cliffs. Press on until the path brings you to the bottom of a road, with several houses edging it.

4 Go through a deer gate on the right and follow the path through young birch woodland. At the Y-junction of paths, keep right and descend gently to another deer gate. Beyond go on along the wide grassy trod, taken at the outset, to rejoin your vehicle.

Practicals

Distance:	2 miles / 3.4 km
Time:	1–2 hours
Map:	OS Landranger 32

35

Kinloch to Leitir Fura

Park in the large well laid out car park in Kinloch Forest, grid ref. 703162. To reach this, leave Broadford, east, and at Skulamus follow the A851. Half a mile south of the turning to Drumfearn, take the left turn at a sign for Leitir Fura. Cross a cattle grid and then a burn on a wooden bridge, and then continue for a mile down the forest track to the car park.

The information board in the car park says that **Kinloch Forest** is one of the finest native woodlands in Scotland, with oak, ash,

Bridge near Leitir Fura

birch, holly, willow, hazel and rowan. Much of the forest was planted with conifers when timber was needed by the nation. Now the Forest Enterprise remit is much wider and takes into consideration conservation and amenity. Here they are engaged in a major project to remove most of the exotic conifers and replace them by allowing natural regeneration of native broadleaves.

The township's name, '**Leitir Fura**', comes from Fura Mhor, the Great Oak, which used to grow on the hillside above the settlement. One summer children of the MacInnes family were playing and accidentally set fire to it and burnt it down. As a result the family were evicted from their home. The woodlands all about were the property of the MacDonalds of Sleat and they employed the people of Leitir Fura to look after them. The tenants were not allowed to cut trees or graze goats. Walls were topped by brushwood to keep out grazing animals. Bark of oak and birch was sold for tanning. Timber was valued for roofing and flooring buildings as well as for boat building, and naturally curved timbers formed the crucks of the roof in the black houses. These dwellings remained the property of the landlord. There were 12 houses and 40–50 people lived here. They abandoned Leitir Fura in the early nineteenth century, for lowland Scotland or North America. There were no forced clearances from this township, just a gradual drifting away from the harsh life of subsistence farming.

Walk 35

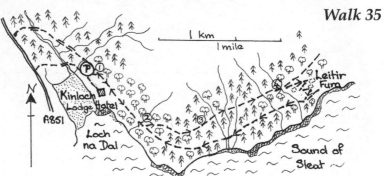

1 Leave the car park by the small gravel path passing a stone and timber 'wigwam', with a light green post signed 'Leitir Fura. Historic Township. 2 miles.' The path zig-zags up to join the forest track, where you turn right. From here you have good views across the bay. Follow the track along the hillside through open birch, oak and rowan. Here you might see siskins feeding on the alder

124

Siskin

cones by the track. Go t
kissing gate beside a barrier
Pass two little quarries on the
on the right, there is an openin
giving lovely views over Isle
its white cottages, pier and lig

2 Take the small path leading off ......,
signed 'Leitir Fura 1½ miles'. This was
an old drovers' path to Kylerhea, where
cattle were driven to swim the sound on
their way to mainland markets. Continue
on to pass through another tall kissing gate.

3 Follow the path as it wends upward through densely planted spruce
to a ride with a burn. Here a marker post indicates a 'short cut'
path off to the right which you ignore. Cross a small ravine on a
stout timber bridge, built by the Welsh Field Squadron of the Royal
Engineers in June 1991. Climb a rise to enter a cleared area from
where there is a wonderful view across to Loch Hourn, the Sound
of Sleat and, opposite, Sandaig—Camusfearna of Gavin Maxwell's
Ring of Bright Water—with its lighthouse island, house and sandy
beaches. Beinn Sgritheall towers behind.

4 Cross another small wooden bridge and at the marker post, where
the path divides, take the right branch, which zig-zags downhill
through ancient ash and hazel. The wood is open and there are
pleasant views across the Sound of Sleat. Go on along the path as
it winds down through the settlement of Leitir Fura to become a
grassy highway as it gets lower. The way then zig-zags down to a
T-junction with a marker post. Turn right along the forest track to
return to the car park.

Practicals

*Type of walk: Easy walking on forestry tracks. Several
openings in the trees allow you to enjoy some very fine views*

Distance: 4 miles / 6.4 km
Time: 2 hours
Map: OS Pathfinder 219 North Sound of Sleat
OS Landranger 33

Kylerhea—The Otter Haven

Park in the Otter haven car park, grid ref. 786212. To reach this take the minor road, signed Kylerhea, which leaves the A87 east of Breakish, between Kyleakin and Broadford.

The Otter Haven lies along the rocky shoreline of the kyle. Here Forest Enterprise, with advice from the Vincent Wildlife Trust, are caring for one of Britain's most thriving otter populations. It is a superb place for otters as it provides them with all their needs. There are good sites for their holts among rocks. There is a plentiful supply of food particularly in the narrows where shoals of fish are almost constantly in passage. But most important is that the shoreline is largely inaccessible and undisturbed by man.

No dogs are allowed on the trail as they can disturb the wildlife of the area simply by leaving their scent.

1 Walk north along the forest track to pass a notice describing the otter haven and where you might also spot the ferry to Glenelg below. Go through the entrance gate. About 1km along the forest track take another narrower track branching right, signed 'Otter Hide'. Follow the path as it descends and then take another path on the right to the hide, where you are asked to be quiet. Enjoy the

Walk 36

excellent view. You will probably spot cormorants, gulls, kittiwakes, gannets, herons, and oyster catchers, as well as seals, porpoises and, of course, otters.

2 Leave the hide and go back up to the path and turn right. The way descends to a burn in a gully, which is lined with birch and rowan, woodrush and ferns. Cross the wooden footbridge below a fall and then follow the way, left, up a wooden staircase beside the burn. Cross the burn again, wind round ascending some more stairs and then rejoin the forest track.

3 Turn right to walk the high level terrace above the kyle. Enjoy the good views as you go. Cross a ravine, full of torrential waterfalls, on an enormous solid girder bridge. Eventually the track comes down to cross below a power line and ends at the burn beyond.

Heron

4 To return keep on the forest track unless you plan a second trip to the hide.

Practicals

Type of walk. This is a pleasant walk, very easy along made up paths and forest tracks. It is a good one for a wet day, when a picnic can be eaten in the shelter of the hide!

Distance:	2½ miles / 4 km
Time:	1 hour plus the time you spend in the hide
Map:	OS Landranger 33
NB:	Don't forget to take binoculars.

37

Broadford Coast

Park in the public parking area at Broadford, grid ref. 643235, in front of the Post Office, Bank, and Information Centre.

Far below the high red- granite peak of **Beinn na Callich**, where legend suggests a Norwegian princess is buried, Broadford Bay curves pleasingly. Here the black shingle shore is backed by low cliffs and a large conifer plantation. Between the cliffs and the trees the land is rough, supporting large tussocks of heather and sometimes tangled willow scrub. Here the land can be wet and ankle wrenching and you may wish to walk the shore where possible. The start of the walk from Broadford is easy and a delight, the middle section can be challenging and the end section, which can be approached from the forest car park, is very pleasing.

Glamaig and Beinn Dearg from Broadford Coast Walk

1 Cross the road from the parking area and walk down a turning signed 'Youth Hostel and An Arcasaid' (anchorage). Bear left at the corner and take the reinforced footpath to the right of the continuing road, with fine views across the bay to the small

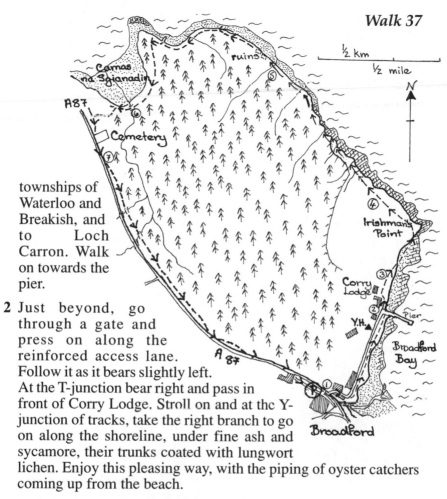

townships of
Waterloo and
Breakish, and
to Loch
Carron. Walk
on towards the
pier.

2 Just beyond, go
through a gate and
press on along the
reinforced access lane.
Follow it as it bears slightly left.
At the T-junction bear right and pass in
front of Corry Lodge. Stroll on and at the Y-
junction of tracks, take the right branch to go
on along the shoreline, under fine ash and
sycamore, their trunks coated with lungwort
lichen. Enjoy this pleasing way, with the piping of oyster catchers
coming up from the beach.

3 Pass a ruined croft and take a grass trod to the right of a gate to
carry on with a wall to your left. The path goes down to the shore,
then up to the top of a low headland, Irishman's Point. Climb a
stile over a fence and follow round a wall corner to go on through
the heather to the shore. Offshore you can see the Crowlin Isles,
Pabay, Longay and the little Guillamon islands. Ahead is the vast
bulk of Scalpay.

4 From now on the way to the next fence, with its broken stile,
becomes more difficult. Beyond, you may prefer to walk along the
shore taking care on slippery basalt slabs until you are forced inland

129

by a higher headland jutting seawards and too difficult to climb. When you spot a large green sward among the heather, aim for this and take a steepish path up the slope behind to avoid the largest and most tedious of the headlands. As you go keep a look out for otters, the indistinct path is littered with their spraints.

5 And then the way improves and you can enjoy views to Scalpay and back towards the Skye Bridge. The distinct path leads you over a little headland, past a pillar of rock and then down to a delightful green area set around several ruined crofts where you will want to pause. From now on the going is easy, along a narrow strip of grass at the shoreline to come to a little bay. Half way round join a forestry track, wide and easy to walk between sitka spruce. Directly above looms shapely Beinn na Caillich.

6 Cross the bridge and then, soon after, take a track forking left. Walk on to a kissing gate, beyond which is a parking area for those who wish to complete just the last section of the coastal walk. Turn left and walk a tiny stretch of the old road leading to the A87. Turn left again to walk the grassy verge of this busy road. Go past a small cemetery. Beyond, look for a slip path down left to the old road.

7 Follow this as it runs parallel with the A-road. Eventually you have to rejoin the verge of the A87. At the second speed restriction sign, cross carefully and walk on to the car park.

Oystercatchers

Practicals

Type of walk: A good walk with a challenging middle section. Both the beginning and the end parts would make pleasing short walks in their own right.

Distance:	5 miles / 8 km
Time:	2–3 hours
Map:	OS Landranger 32

Raasay—Dun Caan

Park at the ferry terminal at Sconser on the A87, grid ref. 525323. There are fewer ferries in winter but still plenty of time to do this walk. No ferries on Sunday.

The summit of **Dun Caan** is not quite as flat as it looks, and has several outcrops of rock dotted around. Boswell must have been quite nifty to dance his jig up here with a local lass! There is a trig point and a cairn and a phenomenal view. Starting from the north you can see the gneiss hump of Rona below, with Rubha Reidh lighthouse on the mainland beyond, and Suilven and Quinag inland. Then there are the Torridon hills, Applecross opposite, Fuar Tholl behind Lochcarron, then Kintail, Beinn Sgritheall and Ladhar Beinn. Directly below on the south-east side is a small lochan and the green pastures of the settlement of Hallaig, a victim of the clearances. Look for fishing boats in the Inner Sound, with the Crowlin Isles behind and the entrance to Loch Carron. You can see Plockton, Kyle of Lochalsh, the Skye bridge and then round to Broadford, with the whole expanse of the Cuillin, Red and Black, behind to the right. Lastly the rest of Skye up to Trotternish.

Dun Caan and Loch na Mna

In **Inverarish** you will pass four long rows of houses that compose much of the village. These were built in the 1914–18 war to house German prisoners who worked the now defunct iron-ore mines. Except for the straightness of the rows of cosy houses nothing now reminds you of how they came to be built.

Walk 38

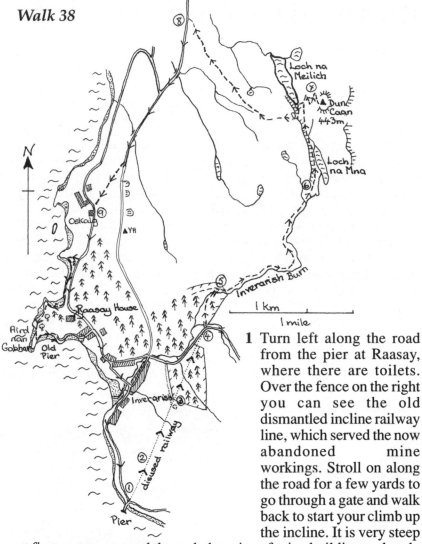

1 Turn left along the road from the pier at Raasay, where there are toilets. Over the fence on the right you can see the old dismantled incline railway line, which served the now abandoned mine workings. Stroll on along the road for a few yards to go through a gate and walk back to start your climb up the incline. It is very steep at first as you proceed through the ruins of mine buildings—but do not be put off as it soon levels out. Keep to the right branch at a fork and go through a small cutting in limestone rock. The grass here is short, sheep-cropped and full of salad burnet and thyme.

2 Beyond the cutting the incline is fenced across but take the gate on the right and continue across the moor, along the grassy way in the midst of heather and bog. Pass a mine building on the right where another (lower) trackbed branches off to the left. Go left to cross this and return to the main track (this slight diversion is necessary because the bridge has gone).

3 Cross the stile into the forest and continue along the track, edged by lodgepole pine, with scots pine and birch on the track. Ignore the waymarked track coming in on the left. Cross a wide ride with a view down to the village of Inverarish, then descend a steep bank. (At this point the railway crossed a deep valley on a viaduct, the pillars of which are still standing—testimony to the skills of the engineers of the day.) Cross the burn and another path, and then climb steeply up the far side onto the railway line again, to pass through birch and rowan on a mossy trackbed. Then the forest opens out. Cross a stile onto the open moor and go on.

4 Where the track converges with the road, cross the latter and go round the left side of a ruined mine building. Pass through a metal gate and cross a wooden decked bridge over the burn. Follow the forest track, (named the Burma Road (BR) as it was built by prisoners of war), through young trees and then more mature. Cross the Inverarish Burn on a stout wooden bridge, with fine waterfalls upstream. Where the BR goes off left, stride ahead to a white ringed post.

5 Turn right, by the post, to climb steps which curve back towards the burn, ascending steeply. The path goes up beside the waterfall, protected on the right by a low stone wall, then a wooden handrail. At the top cross a stile onto the open moor, with the burn to your right and a deer fence to the left. Continue on the often wet but always clear way beside the Inverarish Burn to come to a flatter area and a cairn, with Dun Caan and Loch na Mna now visible ahead.

6 Make your way around the bog to Loch na Mna and follow the continuing path above the west side of the loch shore, keeping below a line of crags. Ascend a clear path which then contours below the cone of Dun Caan until it meets another path coming across from the line of crags. The path up Dun Caan is very clear from here—to the right, arrowed, and zig-zagging up steep cropped grass.

7 After enjoying the spectacular views, retrace your steps downhill. Ignore the contouring path you came up and continue downhill on a long slant into the defile which contains both Loch na Mna and Loch na Meilich. Cross the beach at the head of the latter. At the far side of the defile climb up a long slanting path to the top of the escarpment ahead and then follow a pleasing path across the hill with a lochan to the right and clear views of Beinn Tianavaig in front. Over the next brow you can see the tidal Holoman Island. The final stretch of path delightfully crosses rough rock slabs.

8 At the metalled road, turn left. At a junction, with a triangle of grass in the middle, take the left branch. Cross a bridge, connected to a huge stone wall, which follows an escarpment all the way up the valley. Soon after this take a metal gate, on the right, to a track which you follow downhill. Go on through a tall metal kissing gate and down a grassy slope to the lower road, where you turn left. Enjoy the green pastures which stretch down to the sea, a great contrast from the moorland you have just left.

9 Stride on along the road, walking for about an hour through Inverarish and on to the pier. If you have plenty of time you might wish to divert along the shore by taking a small metal gate on the right where the road enters woodland, and then on round Aird nan Gobhar, a delightful promontory. The path brings you back to the Old Pier, from where a road leads back to join the road to Inverarish. In either case you have the chance to obtain refreshment at the Isle of Raasay Hotel or at the cafe in the Outdoor Centre in Raasay House.

Practicals

Type of walk: An exciting round walk to an exceptional hill. The way, generally on reasonable paths, takes you through forest, over open moor, up to the summit of Dun Caan It returns over moorland and then along a pleasing shoreline, either by road or, by diversions where use of a map would be helpful.

Distance: 10 miles / 16 km
Time: 7–8 hours
Map: The Forestry Commission leaflet shows the paths walked and the OS Landranger 32 would be useful.

Sligachan to Peinchorran

Park on the A87, by the picnic area and camp site, close to the Sligachan Hotel, grid ref. 485301

A mile and a half, from Peinchorran, along the B833, stands the cairn commemorating the **Battle of the Braes**. In the late 1800s crofters were very angry at being unable to use grazing land they believed was rightfully theirs and ceased to pay their rent. Summonses were issued for non-payment of dues but the crofters refused to accept them. On April 17, 1882 fifty policemen from Glasgow appeared and battle began. Whole families met the police forcing them to retreat. Various Scottish newspapers took up the crofters cause and in 1883 a Royal Commission looked into the problems. By 1886 the first Crofters Act was passed giving security of tenure. This encouraged the crofters to build new houses and improve their land without having their rent increased by the landlord.

1 Descend from the parking area to walk through the camp site. Join the good path that runs along the shore of Loch Sligachan and leads through heather and bracken to the Allt Dubh, which is crossed on convenient boulders. Continue on over several more burns.

Monument, Battle of the Braes

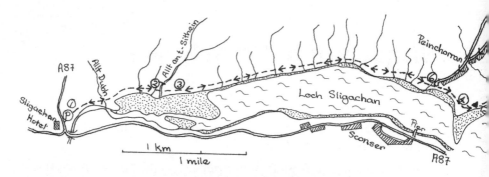

2 Cross below the waterfall on Allt an t-Sithien—this could present problems after heavy rain. (If so you might wish return to your vehicle and drive back towards Portree to take the B883. This narrow road and the path along the shore meet at a small car park at Peinchorran.) Across the water towers conical Glamaig. From now on a better path moves up above the shoreline.

3 Continue on the three-mile path, stepping over the many small streams bisecting the path finally to cross the Allt Garbh Mor. Beyond, the path ascends the slope overlooking Peinchorran. Descend towards the picnic table and the parking area and then move right to the shore.

4 Wind left, following a good track. It soon diminishes to a path through outcrops, with a good view across the Sound of Raasay, where you might see the ferry on its way to and from Sconser. Continue up the path to the top of Torr Beag and go on along a grassy swathe onto Torr Mor to enjoy the spectacular views. Pause here and look for the striking white and black male eiders, shepherding their brown ducks through the choppy water of the Sound, cooing as they go.

Eiders

136

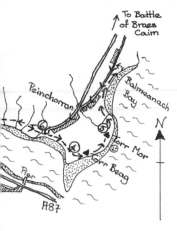

5 When you come to the edge of this little hill, zig-zag down the slopes to the side of a small burn, which you cross on stones. Walk on round Balmeanach Bay on grass between the fence on the left and boulders and pebbles of the shore to your right. At the end of the fence, join a track that winds up, left, to the road. Turn left to return to the little parking area.

Red-throated diver

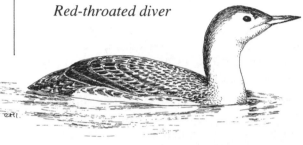

6 If you are unable to be picked up here by a kind friend, return back alongside Loch Sligachan, with superb views of the Cuillin ahead. If you have been dropped off at Sligachan you might wish to catch a bus, to return to Portree. Nicholson Bus Service runs on a Friday at 12.59 and also at 15.59 on schoolday Fridays.

Crowberry

Practicals

Type of walk: This is a good walk for spotting waders and sea birds. If you decide to return by bus, you may wish to walk up the B-road to see the Battle of the Braes cairn.

Distance:	8½ miles / 13.5 km
Time:	5–6 hours
Map:	OS Landranger 32

40

Beinn Tianavaig

Park in a large lay-by, with picnic tables, down by the beach of Tianavaig Bay, grid ref. 508389. To reach this, drive 2 miles south from Portree to take, on the left, the B883 signed 'The Braes'. Then, two miles further on take, also on the left, a minor road signed, 'Camastianavaig'. Turn right at the telephone box.

If you decide to return by the **'landslipped' route** you come steeply down to an idyllic grassy oasis behind a pebble beach, where curlews and oyster catchers mingle and call. There are cultivation ridges behind a huge shingle bank, which is man-made and there are signs of walling where it gets higher. There are house remains beyond it in a further part of the bay.

1 From the picnic area, follow the road towards the north side of the bay, crossing the burn. Continue up to a post box on the right at the point where the road swings round to the left. Go straight ahead up the grassy bank and follow a gap between a shelter belt of spruce on the left and the fence of a garden belonging to the bungalow on the right. There are more cottage gardens beyond,

Beinn Tianavaig

but the gap and the path continue. The path weaves its way along beside the stones of an old wall, under some rowan trees and through a very narrow gap between fences at the top.

2 Go through a space in an old turf dyke and out onto the open hill. Go left round the fence corner just beyond the gap and take a path which slants quite steeply up the hillside, away from the fence. Head for a gap towards the left of a band of rocks above you. Once over this rise, walk towards an obvious rocky knoll on the skyline. The summit of Beinn Tianavaig is over to the left. Watch as you go for a peregrine, a regular visitor here, circling effortlessly over the escarpment.

3 Just before you reach the knoll, turn left and head off over the pleasant short grass towards the summit. Follow the cliff edge upward, along a fairly clear path, with Beinn Tianavaig's own pinnacles below over the edge. Make your way through a break in a line of small cliffs and up to what seems to be the obvious summit. But as is so often the case the real top is some distance further on, with a regular standard issue for Skye—a cylindrical trig point. The summit also has a cairn and patches of mountain everlasting and alpine lady's

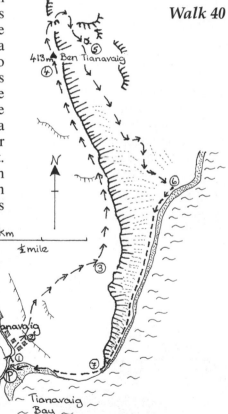

Walk 40

413m ▲ Ben Tianavaig

N

½Km

¼mile

Camastianavaig

~ Tianavaig ~
~ Bay ~

mantle. From here you can see the Storr and in clear weather, Suilven, Quinag, Arkle and Foinaven in Sutherland. You can also see on the mainland, Kintail, Beinn Sgritheall and Ladhar Bheinn. To the north-east, and below, is Portree and its harbour. Down to the right is the topsy-turvy world of the landslip area, with its pinnacles.

4 Now a choice has to be made, either to retrace your outward route down to Camastianavaig or, take the more dramatic and exposed generally pathless way back around the coast. As with all landslipped areas the terrain is confusing and it is worth looking down at your descent route before you try to find it. For the more exposed way, head down north towards the Storr, over sheep-cropped turf. Go round the back of a rocky knoll to come to a col where an obvious path goes down to the right through an old dyke into the 'bowl' below—you are now facing south down the Sound of Raasay. Weave a way through the boulders and little mounds, keeping the main crags to your right.

5 Start to descend steeply towards the sea. The valley goes down almost in a series of steps, where you should avoid the centre full of moss-topped boulders by keeping to the left for easier walking. When well down, head for a little lip with a sharp 'tooth' of rock on your left, then continue down steep grassy slopes to another 'tooth'. Here it is best to traverse round to the left through the heather on sheep tracks to avoid a steep gully. Then head back right and zig-zag down the right bank of the gully to the shore. You will want to pause here awhile.

6 Then take a narrow but pleasant path that sets off back around the headland, just above the shore. It crosses the occasional rockfall from the cliffs above to your right. Climb gradually until the way contours about thirty feet above the beach and the path becomes

Peregrine

little more than sheep tracks. The slope gets steeper and you should allow plenty of time to negotiate it with care. Take the lower path when there is a choice to avoid two nasty earth slips. Eventually you must scramble up to rejoin the higher path before the ground becomes too steep at the headland because

Wood Sorrel

this is the only path which goes round. It passes right up under the rocks and round the cliff at the end of the headland—at one place you have to stoop under an overhang with a drop to your left—but the path is firm and fairly wide and it is not as bad as it sounds.

7 The way then comes out onto the open hillside, with birch and tall aspen trees, below to your left. The cottages of Camastianavaig are ahead, encircling the bay. Follow the path through an old hazel coppice, cross a burn and then follow round the corner of a fence and along the bank at the back of the shore. Go in front of a ruin and then down on to the pebbles to cross the beach to the burn. Go round the corner of a fence and up to the road bridge. Turn left to cross the bridge and return to your car. If the tide is high and the beach is covered, do not go down to the bay but continue on round the hillside behind the houses until you come to the gap in the dyke where you first came out onto the hill, and retrace your steps from there.

Practicals

Type of walk: A most enjoyable hill trek on good grass with superb views. The return by the landslipped area is interesting and brings you down to a lovely peaceful grassy haven by the shore. The way round the headland is airy and white knuckle in parts. If you do NOT like exposed situations, you should just look at the landslipped area and then return to Camastianavaig by your outward route.

Distance: 5 miles / 8 km
Time: 3–4 hours
Map: OS Landranger 23

Clan Walks

A series of walks described by Mary Welsh, covering some of the most popular holiday areas in the Scottish Highlands and Islands.

Titles published so far include:

1. 44 WALKS ON THE ISLE OF ARRAN
2. WALKS ON THE ISLE OF SKYE
3. WALKS IN WESTER ROSS
4. WALKS IN PERTHSHIRE
5. WALKS IN THE WESTERN ISLES
6. WALKS IN ORKNEY
7. WALKS ON SHETLAND
8. WALKS ON ISLAY
9. WALKS ON CANNA, RUM, EIGG & MUCK
10. WALKS ON TIREE, COLL, COLONSAY AND A TASTE OF MULL
11. WALKS IN DUMFRIES AND GALLOWAY

OTHER TITLES IN PREPARATION

Books in this series can be ordered through booksellers anywhere. In the event of difficulty write to Clan Books, The Cross, DOUNE, FK16 6BE, Scotland.